I0112627

Praise for

REVENUEGETTER

"*RevenueGetter* is the playbook every sales leader wishes they'd had on day one. Ryan brings sharp insight and a refreshing dose of honesty to the art of turning managers into coaches and teams into consistent performers. Engaging and grounded in real experience—this is the kind of book that actually moves the needle."

DR. MARSHALL GOLDSMITH, Thinkers50 #1 executive coach and *New York Times* bestselling author of *The Earned Life, Triggers,* and *What Got You Here Won't Get You There*

"Ryan Taft brings an innovator's mindset to sales leadership. *RevenueGetter* shows that the secret to breakthrough performance isn't more pressure—it's more creativity, curiosity, and coaching. Every growth-minded leader should read this book."

JOSH LINKNER, five-time tech entrepreneur and *New York Times* bestselling author of *Disciplined Dreaming* and *Big Little Breakthroughs*

"Ryan Taft gets right to the heart of what separates average managers from transformational leaders: coaching. *RevenueGetter* is a clear, practical road map that will help leaders elevate performance, drive results, and create teams that thrive."

RYAN ESTIS, keynote speaker, entrepreneur, and coauthor of the bestseller *Prepare for Impact*

"Ryan Taft does it again! *RevenueGetter* isn't just another leadership book—it's the real deal. I had so many lightbulb moments. It's equal parts real talk, practical tools, and heart. Ryan somehow takes what we *know* we should be doing as leaders and makes you actually want to do it. Every sales leader needs this book."

AMY DRUHOT, author of *Just Brave It*, keynote speaker, and vice president of sales, Eastwood Homes

"Ryan Taft cuts through the noise with stories, frameworks, and no-nonsense tools that get results. If you lead a sales team and want more than pep talks and quick fixes, *RevenueGetter* is the playbook you've been waiting for."

DAVID NEWMAN, CSP, author of *Do It! Selling* and *Market Eminence*

"I've had the privilege of working with Ryan Taft for over six years, and he is world-class at what he does. He has an unmatched ability to transform sales teams and leadership groups by elevating culture, sharpening habits, instilling work ethic, and driving strategic thinking. *RevenueGetter* captures the essence of his approach—practical, inspiring, relatable, and proven to deliver results. If you want to build a winning sales organization and bring out the best in your people, this book is a must-read."

SHANT SAMTANI, executive vice president of sales, Esperanza Homes

"Ryan's coaching completely reshaped how I approached my career. I was doing well in sales, but I hit a slump. Through the strategies outlined in *RevenueGetter*—consistent tweaks, accountability through daily check-ins, and a focus on the right behaviors—I found the breakthrough I needed. The result? I went on to win the HBACA MAME Salesperson of the Year Award. What makes Ryan stand out isn't just that he knows how to boost sales; it's that he tailors the approach to the individual, showing you exactly how to go from good to great."

CHARLIE PENOVICH, community sales manager, Taylor Morrison

"Few books translate leadership into action as clearly as *RevenueGetter*. Ryan Taft delivers a framework that's honest, practical, and proven to make people better."

MATTHEW DICKS, author of *Storyworthy*

"Ryan Taft has made a tremendous positive impact on our business for both our sales team and our leadership team. His ability to challenge, inspire, and connect on a human level has elevated how we communicate, lead, and perform. With *RevenueGetter*, Ryan offers that kind of impact to the world, capturing the essence of great coaching and showing how unlocking the potential in others ultimately drives growth, alignment, and results."

LINNEA CHAPMAN, corporate vice president of marketing, Trumark Homes

"Ryan Taft has spent his career helping leaders and teams reach their potential. *RevenueGetter* brings his proven framework to life—simple, actionable, and full of heart. It's a powerful guide for anyone who wants to grow people, performance, and profit."

CALEB GUILLIAMS, author of *The AND Asset* and founder and CEO, Better Wealth

"I've known Ryan Taft for a long time, and I can tell you—he's the real deal. The principles Ryan teaches in *RevenueGetter* aren't just words on a page or recycled scripts; they are new, fresh, and proven concepts and frameworks that will truly help you level up in your ability to sell and generate revenue. Ryan is one of those very unique people who leads with heart, challenges with love, and brings out the best in people. This book captures that spirit and gives you the tools to do the same. Get it for you and every leader you know who's ready to make a real impact."

JUSTIN PRINCE, author, speaker, and founder of MAKE Wellness

RYAN TAFT

REVENUE GETTER

How to Build and Coach Sales Teams That Win

www.amplifypublishinggroup.com

RevenueGetter: How to Build and Coach Sales Teams That Win

For more information, please contact:
Amplify Publishing, an imprint of Amplify Publishing Group
620 Herndon Parkway, Suite 220
Herndon, VA 20170
info@amplifypublishing.com

Library of Congress Cataloging-in-Publication Data has been applied for.

CPSIA Code: PRV1125A

ISBN-13: 979-8-89138-935-9

Printed in the United States

For my wife, Melissa—the best coach I know.

Your compassion and genuine care for others set the standard for what true coaching should be.

You love people deeply, yet you hold them accountable to grow into who God created them to be.

CONTENTS

INTRODUCTION ix

CHAPTER ONE
MAKING THE IDENTITY SHIFT FROM MANAGER TO COACH 1

CHAPTER TWO
THE SIX MANAGER STYLES 11

CHAPTER THREE
MICROSKILLS AND THE THREE TYPES OF COACHING SESSIONS 21

CHAPTER FOUR
IDENTIFYING THE MICROSKILLS THAT MATTER 35

CHAPTER FIVE
BUILDING A CULTURE OF COACHING 47

CHAPTER SIX
WHO IS THE COACHING FOR ANYWAY? 55

CHAPTER SEVEN
THE THREE GOALS OF EVERY COACHING SESSION 65

CHAPTER EIGHT
THE 4E COACHING METHOD: EXPLAIN 75

CHAPTER NINE
THE 4E COACHING METHOD: EXHIBIT 83

CHAPTER TEN
THE 4E COACHING METHOD: EXECUTE 93

CHAPTER ELEVEN
THE 4E COACHING METHOD: EVALUATE 109

CHAPTER TWELVE
"DO IT AGAIN!" YOUR THREE NEW FAVORITE WORDS 119

CHAPTER THIRTEEN
TRUST, BUT VERIFY . . . ACTUALLY, JUST VERIFY 127

CHAPTER FOURTEEN
THE CALENDAR DISEASE 139

CHAPTER FIFTEEN
COACHING WHEN IT'S HARD: THE FOUR TOUGHEST PROFILES AND THE FOUR TOUGHEST SCENARIOS 151

CHAPTER SIXTEEN
COACHING SOUNDS GOOD, BUT . . . 165

CHAPTER SEVENTEEN
FROM READING TO REVENUE 175

CONCLUSION 183
HOW TO WORK WITH RYAN 185
ACKNOWLEDGMENTS 189
ABOUT THE AUTHOR 193
READER'S NOTES 195

INTRODUCTION

I don't know about you, but when I made my way into management, I was extremely fortunate to receive an invite to a management school where they taught me how to performance-coach sales reps so they could become the best version of themselves and generate more revenue, make more money, and help our company hit sales and revenue goals.

Uhhh . . . I am 100 percent joking.

I didn't receive one minute of training. Heck, not even one second. It was more of a "You're hired. Go get 'em, Tiger!" Maybe you did have some training on how to coach and train sales reps, but if you're reading this book, odds are high that you didn't.

If you had an experience like mine, you probably found yourself in management needing to get your team to perform better but at a loss on how to get them to do that. So, what do you do? You schedule a one-on-one to let them know they need to make more sales, right? You tell them things like this:

- "We're behind on our goals, so I am going to need you to really push for more sales."
- "Who do you have in the pipeline that you think might convert?"
- "Have you reached into the CRM to see if anyone might be ready to buy?"

Of course, your sales rep says, "I have a few leads I am working." You reply with, "Great! Let me know if you need anything to push them over the edge." And that's it.

Or you get in front of your entire team and announce a killer sales contest that involves spinning a wheel for extra cash or a big trip to Jamaica.

Does any of this sound familiar?

There's one major problem with these approaches: They are short-term fixes, if fixes at all. We resort to these types of pep talks and motivation ploys because of one simple truth: We don't really know what else to do.

"All change begins with telling the truth."—Dan Sullivan

Why I Wrote This Book

To be fairly direct, I wrote this book because there is one major gap in the skill set of managers across the country. That skill is performance coaching.

In 2003, I was a new manager in new home sales, and I couldn't be more excited and scared at the same time. I was working for a Fortune 100 company that was extremely results driven. I was a young manager, and as I mentioned, had zero training on how to manage anyone or anything.

One day, my VP of sales called me into his office and told me that I needed to fix a performance problem. That problem's name was Leslie. What was the problem? Leslie couldn't turn in a sales contract without multiple mistakes. As you could imagine, these constant mistakes cost time and sometimes resulted in cancelled contracts altogether.

Leslie was a veteran salesperson who was always at the top of the leaderboard. If that wasn't intimidating enough, she had been selling longer than I had been alive and, truthfully, scared the crap out of me.

One day, I drove out to Leslie's sales site to fix the problem (her). I was so determined. I recall thinking how I would go through the contract mistakes with her, show her how easy it was going to be to fix the issues, and then Leslie would thank me profusely. I mean, after all, I was just there to help, right?

When I walked into Leslie's office, she was sitting at her desk staring intently at her computer. I was hoping she was writing a contract. That particular day, Leslie was wearing a black long-sleeve top with a black leather skirt and black boots. She had her hair pulled back tightly into a bun that practically guaranteed she would never need Botox. Seriously. On her face were no-rim glasses that had small square lenses.

As I walked into her sales office, she glanced over at me with a look of disdain and said in the most definitive tone, "Whatever it is, I don't have time for it . . . or for you, so you're just going to have to come back."

Let me pause here to share that I really wish this was the part where I tell you that I won Leslie over, helped her with her contract issues, and then got a raise. Well . . . that's not what happened. Instead, I chickened out! I made my way into a model home and spent thirty minutes taking inventory of what light bulbs needed to be changed and where we needed paint touch-ups.

I never did have that coaching session with her.

The truth is I didn't know how to coach her to begin with, and she knew it. I did some serious reflecting after that failed coaching session. Specifically, I reflected back to a lesson from a mentor who shared the most powerful nonbiblical quote I have ever heard:

> "Don't wish it were easier. Wish you were better."
>
> —Jim Rohn

That was when I decided to master the art of performance coaching. Since that time, I have been on a quest to learn how to develop others to reach their potential. If I did the math, it would add up to a quarter of a million dollars I have invested in learning about people, performance, habit building, and motivation.

In this book, I am going to give you what I have spent my life studying and save you the money. You're welcome. Over the last two decades, I have coached and trained thousands of salespeople. Today, I am the founder and chief impact officer of Impact Eighty-Eight™. We spend every day helping sales teams learn how to adopt not just new skills but new habits.

I tell you that not to impress you. But I want you to know there is a pattern to performance improvement. A repeatable process that you can use to help your team become true RevenueGetters!

Who This Book Is For

Maybe I am being a little presumptuous, but I believe anyone in sales leadership will benefit from this book. Even though I will be speaking mostly to the front-line sales manager, VPs and directors need to be able to coach their direct reports as well!

The bottom line is that if you manage anyone, you need this book. I should warn you right here and now, though. This book will not work for the micromanager. So if that's your style and you're sticking to it, you should return this book right now and go get one on how to piss off your team and have a lot of turnover (joking, not joking).

The Quick Tour

Each section of this book builds upon the thoughts and techniques from the prior chapters. In other words, don't skip anything. In fact, I recommend reading this book multiple times. It's amazing how you can catch something new on a second, third, or fourth read-through of a book.

In the pages that follow, I challenge many management techniques and philosophies that will cause you to wonder if I'm crazy. I assure you; I am not crazy. I'm convinced that this book will not only help you generate more revenue, but it will help you be a better leader and enjoy your life more. That being said, stick with me and keep an open mind.

The first section is all about defining what a great sales leader is and what a great sales leader does. Specifically, we will redefine your role so that you see yourself as a coach rather than a manager. We will look closely at the six manager identities that people default into and why they are unable to succeed like a RevenueGetting manager does.

Then, we will dive into the three different types of coaching sessions and why microskills are where the magic happens.

If you were hoping for tactical application, you're in luck. We will be getting into the nitty-gritty on how to determine which microskills each of your team members needs to work on by examining the tools and resources you have available to you to help develop a coaching plan.

Next, we get into the mechanics and methodology of a coaching session. Specifically, we will look at four coaching steps to improve your team's performance:

1. Explain
2. Exhibit
3. Execute
4. Evaluate

The last part of the book delves into the challenges and possibilities you may encounter as you transform your role from manager into coach. We will look at how to structure your calendar so you have the time for it, and we will address the real-world obstacles that could hinder you from becoming a true RevenueGetter! After all, we don't want this book to be just another one gathering dust on the shelf, which I affectionately refer to as "shelf-help."

At the back of the book, you'll find some blank notebook-style pages. As you read and come across ideas, tools, and frameworks that you'll want to remember and apply, I encourage you to use that space to capture what stands out and revisit it to turn what you learn into lasting change.

My Promise to You

I've sat in so many trainings where I got nothing out of it, and, on top of that, the experience was like watching paint dry. If you've ever been in one of my live sessions, you know that's not how I roll. I say that because this book is written in an approach similar to the way I present.

I'll share a ton of true stories from the field along with perspectives outside my own. In other words, I won't make up stuff. I have too many real examples to do that!

Lastly, my promise is that if you put into action what's in the following pages, you'll have the skills to train and coach a sales team that closes more deals. Period.

Enjoy!

CHAPTER ONE

MAKING THE IDENTITY SHIFT FROM MANAGER TO COACH

The growth and development of people is the highest calling of leadership.

—Harvey S. Firestone

In June 2015 I had a coaching call with a sales leader, who I will call Stan, that I will never forget. It was the day that I realized why sales leaders don't get in the field to coach their teams. Prior to this call, I would have blamed lack of knowledge or perhaps lame meetings as the main culprit. But that day I realized sales leaders could have clear calendars and all the training on how to coach, but without this one thing, they won't coach. What was it?

The belief that coaching is their *primary* job.

On the call, I asked Stan, "How is the team doing with the new content we covered in our live session last month?"

Stan hemmed and hawed by saying, "Oh, they're doing pretty good." I knew right in that moment that Stan had not coached one single person.

Rather than chastise Stan, I decided to ask him a few clarifying questions. I said, "Stan, how many one-on-one coaching sessions did you do in the last three weeks?"

He replied, "Well, I've had a couple of conversations with team members, and we had a really great sales rally!"

I paused and then said, "You didn't do any coaching sessions, did you?"

Stan's voice got quiet, and he replied, "Well . . . no, not really." I could tell he was embarrassed, and I didn't want him to feel like I was catching him doing something wrong. I asked him to share why he didn't really get to any of the coaching sessions. His reply blew me away. He said, "Well, I'd love to coach people, but that's not really my primary role." When I asked him to share what he believed his primary role was, Stan said, "To manage processes, open new communities, hire and fire, and set up pricing."

You see, Stan's issue wasn't an issue of capability or desire. His issue was that he believed his job was about the direction of managing processes more so than developing people. From that point on, our coaching calls were focused on changing his belief about what his job role was.

That's the point of this chapter . . . to shift your belief, or your identity, to that of a coach.

Leader as Coach

I want you to think about who your best team member is. I don't mean the one who makes the most sales alone. I'm talking about the one who hits sales quotas, is a problem-solver, is low maintenance, and is enjoyable to work with.

Now think about your worst team member. If you could duplicate one of them, which one would you duplicate? If you're not a weirdo, you likely said you'd duplicate your easy, productive team member, right? It would be great to be able to hire a bunch of people who had all the right qualities and skills, but that's just not reality. So, it's fair to say that you are going to have to develop those skills and habits to have a team that operates on all cylinders.

In the following chapters, I am going to give you the tools and skills to develop your team, but you need to know, right here and now, that this is your primary job. As a leader, you are a coach first and foremost.

When you focus on developing your team's skills, there are some inherent benefits:

- Fewer problems to have to handle
- More fun on the job
- A self-managing team
- Fewer late-night phone calls

But here are the two major benefits of developing your team:

- More sales
- More revenue

Key Skills + Mastery = Additional Revenue

Death by Meeting

I am a huge fan of Patrick Lencioni. In particular, his book *Death by Meeting* had a profound impact on me.

I recall in 2004, I was sitting in an all-day manager meeting (#punchmeintheface). I remember thinking, "Why the heck does this meeting take all freaking day long?" I knew that I could have been more productive out in the field. Instead, we were in an all-day meeting "talking" about how to make more sales instead of coaching our sales team to make more sales!

The meeting was led by our new VP of sales, Stacy. Stacy was from the South and had the twang in her voice to prove it. Lucky for me, Stacy was looking for ways to shake up the routine from the prior sales VP.

Management is not the direction of people, it's the development of people.

This all-day meeting was a part of the old leader's legacy. At the lunch break, I pulled Stacy aside and told her I was going out to the field to go get some more sales. She looked at me like I had lost my mind. She said, "But we aren't done with our meeting."

I looked right at her, knowing I could lose my job, and said, "I know. Call me if you need me." With that, I walked out of the building and headed to the field to get more revenue rather than talk about how to get more revenue.

That was the day I became a RevenueGetter. Frankly, it's why my company, Impact Eighty-Eight, has the tag line "A Performance Improvement Company." I truly believe that to get more revenue in the door, you must improve your team's performance.

The Core Mindset of a RevenueGetter

The ultimate goal of this book isn't just to give you strategies, tools, or scripts; it's to help you take on a new professional identity.

In my sales seminars, I often say that management is not the direction of people, it's the development of people.

That's not just a clever line. It's the foundation of everything you'll read in this book.

The promise of *RevenueGetter* is simple: if you make this shift, you will learn to coach your team in a way that builds skills, drives sales, and creates lasting performance improvement. But that only happens if you decide . . . right here, right now . . . to embrace these nonnegotiable mindsets:

1. My job is to coach my team consistently, not when I have time, not when numbers dip, but as a daily discipline.

2. I will measure performance improvement relentlessly because what gets measured gets improved, and guessing is not a strategy.
3. I will inspire my team intentionally . . . knowing that my words, actions, and example set the emotional climate for the entire sales floor.
4. I will protect our culture fiercely, guarding against complacency, negativity, and anything else that erodes performance or morale.

These aren't "nice to haves." They are the DNA of a true RevenueGetter. If you adopt them, your team will feel it. Your results will reflect it. And your career will never be the same.

The Revenue Formula

Prior to Impact Eighty-Eight, I worked with Shore Consulting, led by Jeff Shore. In 2023, Jeff released a YouTube video where he taught what he calls the Revenue Formula.* Here is that formula:

Revenue = Price x Traffic x Conversion

I won't reteach it here—you can find it easily online if you want to watch it in its entirety—but what I will say is that if you have a certain revenue goal and you aren't hitting it, you have three options:

1. Increase your prices.
2. Increase your traffic.

* Jeff Shore Real Estate Sales Training, "The Revenue Formula: Price x Traffic x Conversion – 5-Minute Sales Training," YouTube, August 19, 2023, https://www.youtube.com/watch?v=UzpkscjbSIU.

3. Increase your conversion rate.

Perhaps you could do all three of these. My observation over the last twenty-five years is that you can only raise prices so much before you create a pricing barrier. As far as traffic goes, you could increase traffic to a certain extent, but there is likely a cap on that as well. But if I ask you if your sales team is maximizing every sales opportunity, odds are high that you would say, "We could be doing better."

By focusing on increasing your conversion rates, you will increase your revenue by the greatest amount without more ad spend or discounting your product to win the sale.

Conversion Case Study

Let's say you sell high-end luxury watches through an online and in-store retail model. Here are your current numbers:

- Price per watch: $10,000
- Monthly traffic: 1,000 qualified shoppers
- Conversion rate: 2 percent (20 sales per month)

Revenue: $10,000 x 20 sales = $200,000/month
Now let's see what happens when you adjust each lever:

1. **Increase Traffic by 20%**
   New Traffic = 1,200 shoppers
   Conversion Rate = still 2% = 24 sales
   Revenue: $10,000 x 24 = $240,000
   Result: $40K gain

2. **Increase Price by 5%**
   New Price = $10,500
   Traffic = 1,000 shoppers

Conversion Rate = still 2% = 20 sales
Revenue: $10,500 x 20 = $210,000
Result: $10K gain

3. **Increase Conversion Rate by 2 Points (from 2% to 4%)**
Traffic = 1,000 shoppers
Conversion Rate = 4% = 40 sales
Revenue: $10,000 x 40 = $400,000
Result: $200K gain

Summary
+20% more traffic = +$40K
+5% price increase = +$10K
+2% conversion rate increase = +$200K

Once again, improving conversion rate drives the largest revenue gain, without more marketing spend or risking customer resistance to higher prices.

Why does this matter so much? Well, if you have been in leadership for any length of time, you're probably familiar with the following typical conversation with a salesperson:

Steve the Sales Leader: "So John, we are down on sales and need to make something happen pretty quick. What do you need to make it happen?"

John: "Well, I feel that if I had a little more back-pocket money or a better incentive, that might get us a couple of deals. I know the Hinkley family would likely convert."

Steve: "Okay. Let me see if I can make that happen. Anything else?"

John: "Yeah . . . the traffic has really sucked recently. It's also been kinda slow. If you could tell marketing to change things up and get me more qualified traffic, that would totally help. These people I am talking to are a waste of time."

Steve: "Roger that. I'll see what I can do."

Steve runs off to save the day by decreasing revenue with a larger incentive for John and convinces marketing to increase their efforts to make more sales. But Steve never stopped and looked at John's conversion efforts. No skill development or coaching at any level. Steve is not a RevenueGetter. Steve is a RevenueLoser.

The point of this book is for you to look at increasing your team's conversion efforts first! Believe me when I tell you there are sales that are left on the table because you aren't converting at the highest levels possible. And if you are converting at the highest levels possible, I am curious as to why you are reading this book. Maybe your VP or company president is making you read it. In that case, sorry, not sorry.

The Payoff

Reread the quote at the beginning of this chapter by Harvey S. Firestone. The payoff is fulfillment and legacy. Yes, getting more revenue is the immediate payoff, but it's way more than that.

I cannot tell you how many people I have coached who are now division presidents, company owners, top salespeople, and more. Watching someone reach their full potential is what it's all about.

Let me share a great example of this. In the spring of 2002, I was running a new-hire class for a Fortune 100 home builder. In that class was a young man by the name of Brian Raab. Brian was a bartender at a swanky club in the Biltmore area of Phoenix.

Brian had a dream of opening up a series of restaurants in the Phoenix area and was looking at selling homes as a way to create a little capital to get that dream started. I had many coaching sessions with Brian, and sure enough, he became a top producer at our company.

I am not one of those coaches who claims responsibility for someone's success, but I know that I likely had an influence on Brian. Brian left our company in 2006 to chase his dream. Today, Brian owns and operates multiple award-winning restaurants in the Phoenix area, including The Mission and The Fat Ox. He also just launched his own tequila brand.

I am so proud of that dude. The fact that I might have influenced his success is worth more than any monetary reward I could imagine.

It's true—growth and development of others is the highest calling.

How do you accomplish that? You become a coach and a RevenueGetter!

Summary

At the heart of this chapter is a simple but powerful truth: Sales leaders don't avoid coaching because they're too busy or lack training; they avoid it because they don't believe it's their primary role. Stan's story made that point impossible to ignore. Until you shift your identity to "leader as coach," all the tools, techniques, and free time in the world won't get you into the field developing your people. The leaders who consistently drive revenue, prevent problems, and build high-performing teams are the ones who treat coaching not as an occasional activity but as the central focus of their role.

When you commit to coaching as your primary responsibility, your priorities become sharper and your impact grows. You stop relying on short-term fixes like discounts or more traffic and instead focus on improving the one factor with the biggest payoff . . . conversion! Over time, you'll see your people achieve more than they thought possible, often surpassing even their own expectations. The reward is more than sales and revenue; it's the legacy of having developed others into leaders, top performers, and success stories. That starts with a belief shift: You are not just a manager of processes; you are a coach and a RevenueGetter.

Questions to Ponder

- What percentage of your time each week is spent managing processes versus developing people? (Be honest. This is about self-awareness, not perfection.)
- If your team's conversion rate improved by 10 percent, what impact would that have on your revenue and your leadership reputation?
- What limiting beliefs about your role as a leader might be holding you back from embracing the identity of a coach? (For example: "I'm too busy," "Coaching is HR's job," "It's faster to fix problems myself.")

Before we dive into the skills and tools in the next chapters, take a moment to assess your current leadership identity. Are you operating as a manager or a coach? Scan the QR code below or visit **RevenueGetter.com/tools** to find out how you rank.

CHAPTER TWO

THE SIX MANAGER STYLES

Leadership is not about being in charge.
It's about taking care of those in your charge.

—Simon Sinek

As we established in the introduction, most sales leaders don't receive any training on how to effectively coach their teams. That being the case, managers tend to default into five alternative leadership styles. I know the chapter title says six. We will get to the sixth one, but first, let's get into the five incorrect styles.

With each and every style, I am going to share with you the challenges that each will have in becoming a RevenueGetter through coaching.

Style #1: The Buddy

This manager holds the belief that if the salesperson likes me, they will perform for me. The manager will try to hang out with the salesperson outside of work and have a personal relationship beyond the office.

I am not saying personal relationships are necessarily bad, but it isn't a strategic performance improvement style. It's more of a hope style. In other words, I hope you like me well enough to hit your goals.

As the late, great business philosopher Jim Rohn used to say, hope is not a strategy.

The downside of this leadership style is that it makes it super awkward for everyone when the salesperson isn't performing. The sales leader will avoid confrontational talks and coaching sessions. Forget challenging the salesperson beyond their own beliefs and capabilities. To the Buddy, this would seem pushy.

Here's a typical conversation between a salesperson and the Buddy:

> **Stephanie (the Buddy):** "Hey, Angie. I could really use your help. Margie is all over me to get some more sales from you. You think you could help a sister out?"
>
> **Angie:** "Well, I mean, sure. But let her know I am doing everything I can out here. What else do you want me to do?"
>
> **Stephanie:** "I know you are . . . and I told her. Don't shoot the messenger. Just do what you can. I would really appreciate it."
>
> **Angie:** "Okay. Will do."
>
> **Stephanie:** "Oh . . . I forgot to tell you I found a new spot for happy hour. You want to go tonight?"
>
> **Angie:** "Totally."

Style #2: The Server

These managers are always bringing coffee and lunch to their salespeople. They hold the belief that if they serve their team, their team will serve them (with sales) in return. I don't disagree with the thinking here. It's actually called the Law of Reciprocity. As Robert Cialdini states in his book *Influence*,

> The [reciprocity] rule says that we should try to repay, in kind, what another person has provided us.

The challenge is twofold. First, we are training our team that to get sales, they should get something first. In fact, I saw this in action yesterday. I was walking my dogs along with a neighbor named Trish. Trish has an older lab mix named Nikki. Nikki has figured out that if she stops walking, Trish will give her a treat to get her moving. So, what does Nikki do every ten feet? She stops! I told Trish someone is getting trained, and it isn't the dog.

The second issue is you aren't working on skill development at all. Again, I am not against bringing my team the occasional coffee or lunch. Just make sure it doesn't become the trigger for action.

Style #3: The Savior

I find the Savior to be the most common of the styles. The reason I say this is because it feels like you are coaching and converting sales.

Here's the typical scenario: You go to do a coaching session with your salesperson. You might even have a plan on what you will coach them on. So far, you're on track. Then, you get into the session with your salesperson and he or she says, "Oh . . . I am so glad you are here. I have an issue that I could really use your help with. You see, the Lechter family has an issue with how the discount was applied, and they have some questions. Could you talk with them really quick? I think they need to hear from someone above me."

And the next thing you know, you are saving the day handling the problems of your sales team. Feels good, but it isn't. Again, I am not saying you won't have these types of scenarios to deal with, but the Savior mistakes coaching with saving the day; therefore, they never actually get to coaching.

When I first was promoted into management, I recall scheduling a meeting with my division president to get some guidance on how to handle a specific scenario. My DP, named Steve, was an intimidating and hugely successful man. In fact, he went on to become one of the most successful COOs in home building.

Steve stood roughly six feet two and always dressed to the nines. His suits likely cost more than I made in a year. He looked like the head of a Wall Street firm that someone would make a movie about.

Walking into his huge corner office, I approached him as he sat behind his massive mahogany desk. Steve looked at me and said, "Hello, Ryan. What can I help you with today?"

I can't recall my exact issue, but what I do recall is how Steve helped me. In fact, it was one of the most valuable leadership lessons I ever received. After I told Steve my issue, I asked him what I should do.

Steve looked at me and paused. He then stood up and said, "Come sit in this chair." I must have looked extremely confused as Steve repeated himself with a little more direction in his tone. "Come sit here."

I cautiously moved over to Steve's chair and sat. He then sat in the chair I had been sitting in. Then came the lesson. He said, "You are now the acting division president. You have all the authority to make decisions. That being said, what would you tell you if you were president?"

I gave Steve some thoughts, which he agreed with, and then he said, "What else?" I gave a little more, and he course-corrected me without giving me the answer. I recall thinking in the moment that Steve was acting like a living version of the bumpers they use for little kids when they go bowling for the first time.

Finally, we came to an answer to my problem, and Steve said something I will never forget. As I was walking out of his office, he said, "Hey, Taft, one more thing. Don't ever come to me unarmed ever again. My job isn't to do your thinking for you. My job is to turn you into a leader. Next time, bring three possible solutions with you, and I will help you pick the right one."

In other words, train people how to think and problem-solve, and they won't be dependent on you.

Style #4: The Slave Driver

This is quite possibly the worst management style out there. Largely driven by ego, this style loves to command people. Often micromanagers and know-it-alls, these folks don't coach at any level.

I had a sales director and sales manager that the team unaffectionately referred to as the Emperor and Darth Vader. I recall the Darth Vader manager answering his phone in front of me by looking at his caller ID, sighing, and answering by saying, "This better be good." #whatajerk

I would like to believe that this style has finally died, but I know they're out there. Odds are extremely high this isn't you. These folks wouldn't touch this book with a ten-foot pole.

Since the Slave Drivers are ego driven, they don't have any patience. A RevenueGetting coach requires patience, as you will see in the following chapters. This requirement excludes these folks from being coaches.

Style #5: The Ghost

This style isn't anywhere to be found. They aren't in the field or on the sales floor coaching anyone. They seem busy, but no one is sure what they are busy doing. Could they become coaches? Possibly.

This type of leader may not be ghosting the entire team. They might be ghosting a portion of the team. They may be ghosting the top performers because they supposedly don't need coaching or the middle performers because they aren't in serious trouble. Perhaps the Ghost disappears on the bottom third of performers because they're going to be replaced anyway. I will address that thinking in chapter 5.

In 2023, I had a conversation with a division president in Phoenix for a major home builder. She asked me how I thought her sales leaders were performing. Secretly, I was ecstatic that she asked. I asked her how much her managers were making, to which she replied, "About $175K." I then asked her how much the average admin employee earned. She shared, "Between $50K and $60K."

I suggested to the DP that she should fire the two managers and hire two more admin folks. With a look of surprise, she asked me, "Why?" I told her that was what they were doing. They weren't in the field at all. They were simply running reports and working from home 100 percent of the time.

Today, those "managers" are no longer working there. They ghosted the sales team, so the company ghosted them.

• • •

Those are the five styles you'll want to steer clear of. Before we move on, take a moment to reflect . . . Do any of those tendencies show up in your own leadership? Be honest with yourself, because recognizing those habits is the first step to replacing them. With that awareness in mind, you'll have a clear contrast for the sixth and final style: the one that drives performance, builds people, and fuels long-term success—the Coach.

Style #6: The Coach

Obviously, this is the style we all should aspire to use. This style is all about developing their team. They prioritize coaching, as is proven on their calendar.

This is also a rare find in the field, and not because of lack of desire. Mainly, managers aren't true coaches for reasons I have already stated. They aren't taught how to coach, their organization doesn't see the value in coaching, or the ROI isn't fast enough.

Let me reassure you this is the category to strive for. It's the most rewarding category, and it is how you boost revenue long-term. As they say in church, if you build the people, the people build the church. The same is true here: If you build the salespeople, the salespeople build the revenue ladders.

How Do You Know Which Style You're Using?

There are two simple ways to find out.

First, take the RevenueGetter Coaching Style Assessment at RevenueGetter.com/tools. It will give you a quick snapshot of which style you most naturally default to today. Once you've completed the assessment, jot down your dominant style in the space below. Awareness is the first step toward growth.

My coaching style today is: ______________________________

Second, pay close attention to the language you use with your team. The words and phrases you choose reveal far more about your leadership style than you might think. Compare what you typically say to the examples of Coach Language provided on page 18. Do you sound more like the Buddy, the Server, the Savior, the Slave Driver, or the Ghost—or do your words reflect the mindset of a true Coach?

Words They Use	
The Buddy	"I hope you can help me hit my numbers."
The Server	"Here's your coffee. Let me know if there's anything you need!"
The Savior	"I'll handle this for you."
The Slave Driver	"I expect results. Just get it done."
The Ghost	Says nothing because they aren't there!

Words a Coach Uses	
The Coach	"Let's take a look at what's working and where you can stretch this month. I believe you're capable of more. Let's get after it."
	"I'm here to support you, but my job is to help you grow. What skill or area would you like to focus on improving this week?"
	"Walk me through how you've handled it so far and what options you see. I'll help you think through your next move."
	"Let's set clear expectations, and then I want to help you build the skills and confidence to deliver those results."
	"I'll be in the field with you this week. Let's spend time together reviewing opportunities and sharpening your approach."

Summary

Most sales leaders step into their roles with little to no training on how to coach effectively. Left to figure it out on their own, many default into one (or more) of the five common manager styles covered in this chapter: the Buddy, the Server, the Savior, the Slave Driver, or the Ghost. While these styles often come from good intentions, they ultimately hinder the development of the team and the consistent growth of revenue.

Your goal, if you want to become a true RevenueGetter, is to consciously move toward the sixth style: the Coach. Coaching isn't about pleasing, saving, or commanding your team. It's about helping them think, act, and perform at a higher level. It's about developing people in a way that drives results and builds their long-term capabilities. No manager stumbles into this style accidentally; it takes intention and practice. The next chapters will begin equipping you with exactly that.

Questions to Ponder

- Which of the five ineffective styles do you see in yourself today? Where is it showing up?
- When your team interacts with you, do they feel developed or merely managed?
- What is one tangible step you can take this month to start showing up more as a Coach and less as one of the default styles?

CHAPTER THREE

MICROSKILLS AND THE THREE TYPES OF COACHING SESSIONS

Mastery is built in the margins—when we focus on the smallest skills, we unlock the biggest results.

—Unknown

Now that we've identified the kind of manager we don't want to be, let's shift gears and unpack what coaching actually is . . . and how to do it effectively.

In his book *Talent Is Overrated*, author Geoff Colvin makes a compelling argument: Top performers aren't born; they're built. Through his research, Colvin discovered that what separates superstars from everyone else isn't raw talent but something called *deliberate practice*.

Although we'll dig deeper into the concept of practice in chapter 12, it's important to introduce Colvin's five key elements of deliberate practice here. They give us a framework for understanding the true role of a coach and why focusing on microskills is so powerful.

According to Colvin, deliberate practice is

- specific and goal driven,
- mentally demanding,

- not inherently enjoyable,
- feedback-rich, and
- usually guided by a coach or expert.*

Let's pause on that first point: *specific*. This is where most coaching breaks down. When we say specific, we mean micro. Not "get better at follow-up," but "craft a stronger opening line in your voicemail." Not "ask better questions," but "replace yes/no questions with open-ended ones." Specific coaching focuses on one targeted skill at a time; it zooms in, not out.

And this is where many sales leaders unintentionally go off course.

Rather than coaching one microskill at a time, they overtrain their team by throwing too much change at them all at once. I'll never forget a meeting I sat in back in 2002. Four different departments were lined up to present to the sales team. #boring!

Each one got up and dumped a new "must-do" on the group. First, it was a new contract addendum. Then a change to how homes were added to the MLS (Multiple Listing Service). After that, an updated SOP. And so on.

Now let me ask you, do you think the sales team nailed the contract addendum the following week? How about the MLS update? The reality? Almost no one implemented any of it.

And when managers were asked why, the usual response was something like, "I don't know. We told them what to do."

That's the problem with a macro-change approach: It overwhelms people. It's too much, too fast, and without the structure of deliberate practice and focused coaching, it almost always falls flat.

Slow down in order to go fast.

---

* Geoff Colvin, *Talent Is Overrated: What Really Separates World-Class Performers from Everybody Else* (Portfolio, 2008).

The Power of One Thing

Slow down in order to go fast.

Think about a time when you had to learn a complex skill, maybe riding a bike, playing the guitar, or driving a car. How did you start? Did you just hop on the bike and pull off a wheelie? Pick up the guitar and nail the song "Little Wing" (the Stevie Ray Vaughan version)? Probably not.

Like most people, you started small. You learned in increments, piece by piece, building confidence and competence one step at a time.

I remember when I first learned how to play T-ball. It was the late '70s, and my coach, Coach Jensen, had the mustache and the shorts to prove it. A fashion disaster? Absolutely. But a great coach? Without question.

Our first practice was at Studio City Park in Studio City, California. Coach Jensen gathered all of us around home plate. "This is home plate," he said. Some of us nodded like we knew; others clearly had no clue.

Then he said, "You stand here and hit the baseball off the tee. Let me show you." He grabbed a bat, teed up the ball, and took a swing.

Next, he placed another ball on the tee and asked, "Where are we?"

We shouted, "Home plate!"

"And what do we do here?"

"Hit the ball!" we yelled.

He smiled and swung again.

Then he had us line up. One by one, each kid grabbed a bat, pointed to the ground, and said, "This is home plate!" then took a swing.

Here's the key: We didn't run the bases. We didn't talk about scoring runs or fielding ground balls. On day one, all we did was learn where to stand and how to swing. That was it.

That's microskill development.

It's focused, intentional, and narrow by design. Just like Coach Jensen, great sales coaches zero in on the fundamentals and isolate one small skill at a time. That's how real learning (and real performance improvement) happens.

What Are Microskills?

So, what exactly are microskills? To define them accurately, we must look at the definition of both parts of the term. According to Dictionary.com, *micro* is very small in comparison with others of its kind.[*] According to Britannica, the word *skill* is defined as the ability to do something that comes from training, experience, or practice.[†] When you put the two definitions together, you get:

Microskill (noun): A very small, specific ability or behavior that comes from training, experience or practice; it is one component of a larger, more complex skill set.

As a point of comparison, look at this list of differences between micro and macroskills:

	Microskills	Macroskills
Scope	Narrow and specific	Broad and complex
Focus	One behavior at a time	Outcome or process oriented
Training	Drill based and repetitive	Situational and holistic
Example	Hit the ball off the tee	Win the game

* Dictionary.com, "micro," accessed September 3, 2025, https://www.dictionary.com/browse/micro.

† *Britannica Dictionary*, "skill," accessed September 3, 2025, https://www.britannica.com/dictionary/skill.

Look at the differences in the table on page 24 and ask yourself, Which side do I tend to lean toward in my coaching—micro or macro? If you said micro, congratulations! You are a rare bird. My experience in watching sales leaders in the field is they almost always lean toward macroskills.

The question is: Why should you adopt microskill development at all?

A Microlearning Success Story

American Tire Distributors (ATD), the world's largest tire distributor, recognized the need to enhance their sales team's training to maintain a competitive edge in the evolving automotive and tire service industry. While initial sales training was provided to new hires, ongoing development was inconsistently reinforced by managers.

In 2016, ATD appointed Rebecca Sinclair as chief people officer to revamp the company's HR and learning strategies. Identifying the limitations of traditional training methods, Sinclair introduced Axonify, a microlearning platform delivering three- to five-minute daily lessons tailored to individual learning needs. This approach aimed to make learning convenient and habitual for employees.

The implementation began with a pilot program focusing on the company's sales-force model.* Within two to three weeks, participants exhibited significant knowledge improvement, which was sustained in subsequent evaluations. Encouraged by these results, ATD rolled out the platform companywide in mid-2017. The learning team collaborated with business leaders to develop relevant content, ensuring alignment with organizational priorities.

---

* Sarah Fister Gale, "Case Study: American Tire Distributors Shares Its Microlearning Success Story," Chief Learning Officer, 2025, https://www.chieflearningofficer.com/2019/12/12/american-tire-distributors-shares-its-microlearning-success-story/?utm.

The microlearning initiative yielded impressive outcomes: Over 90 percent of the sales team engaged with the platform on eighteen out of twenty business days per month. Notably, the top 25 percent of sellers were among the most active users, while the bottom 25 percent engaged the least. For instance, targeted training on a specific manufacturer's products led to a 5.5 percent sales increase, with an estimated 15 percent of that growth directly attributed to improved product knowledge.

Buoyed by this success, ATD expanded the microlearning program to operations and maintenance teams and introduced a paid version, Spark for Retail, offering customers access to the training. This initiative not only enhanced internal performance but also created a new revenue stream, demonstrating the broader business impact of effective microlearning strategies.

The Three Types of Coaching Sessions

What is the biggest reason a macroskill focus dominates? Very simply, managers don't have the time . . . or so they think. I will shoot you straight here. Microskill coaching takes more time. No question about that. That being said, you have to work smarter, not harder, right? The question is: How do you do that?

I am glad you asked. Depending on the number of direct reports you manage, you might be able to do one-on-one coaching with every single person once a week. That would be my preference, but I know that isn't always doable. Without adding an eighth day to the week, you have to get strategic with the time you do have.

With that being said, you will want to leverage the following three types of coaching sessions to make sure each team member is getting a form of microskill coaching.

Coaching Session #1: One-on-One

As I've mentioned, one-on-one coaching is the ultimate form of coaching. Just like people pay top dollar for personal trainers, acting coaches, or private batting lessons for their kids, the value comes from one thing: 100 percent focused attention on performance improvement.

This type of coaching allows you to zero in on specific skill gaps and tailor development to the individual salesperson. The impact goes beyond just improving results; it also builds trust, accountability, and a stronger relationship. After all, relationships grow when you invest time in helping someone become the best version of themselves.

Yes, one-on-one coaching takes more time, but the payoff is worth it. Just remember it's not a "one-and-done" activity. Effective one-on-one coaching requires a strategic follow-up loop with intentional exercises, clear accountability, and a bit of healthy discomfort to drive growth.

We will dive into the specific steps of a one-on-one coaching session in chapters 8 through 11.

One-on-One Case Study

As of this writing, swimmer Michael Phelps is the most decorated Olympian of all time. Of course, he didn't start out that way. When Phelps was eleven years old, all he had was some raw talent and tons of energy. He then met the man who would coach him to twenty-three gold medals, Bob Bowman.

Bowman saw greatness in Phelps and gave him more than some instruction on how to swim better. Bowman invested in Phelps for over twenty years. When I say "invested" in him, I mean he developed Phelps as an athlete and as a human. And his approach wasn't always gentle.

"My job wasn't to be his friend," Bowman would later say. "It was to help him become everything he was capable of becoming."

Here are just a few of the ways Bowman poured effort into Michael Phelps:

Professionally (Performance and Skill Development)

- Identified potential early—recognized Phelps's physical gifts and competitive mindset at age eleven.
- Instilled elite-level discipline—designed grueling training schedules, including twice-a-day practices, 365 days a year (yes, even on holidays).
- Built technical mastery—sharpened Phelps's mechanics, starts, turns, and stroke efficiency with relentless detail.
- Used mental rehearsal—taught Phelps visual techniques and goal-setting habits to prepare for every scenario.
- Prepared him for adversity—simulated race-day setbacks (e.g., goggles filling with water) so Phelps could adapt under pressure.
- Pushed him past limits—constantly raised the bar with personalized challenges and "stretch goals."
- Managed long-term performance cycles—structured training and rest around Olympic cycles to peak at the right moments.
- Developed race strategy—helped Phelps become not just physically dominant but tactically smart in the water.

Personally (Mindset, Growth, and Life Coaching)

- Taught emotional control—helped Phelps manage frustration, fear, and pressure (crucial for high-stakes competition).

- Held him accountable—never let Phelps off the hook; challenged excuses and reinforced personal responsibility.
- Provided structure and stability—became a steady presence during Phelps's turbulent teenage years and early fame.
- Guided him through struggles—supported Phelps during battles with anxiety, depression, and post-Olympic identity loss.
- Modeled professionalism—showed what it meant to pursue excellence with consistency, preparation, and class.
- Encouraged leadership—helped Phelps transition from solo competitor to team leader in later Summer Olympic Games.
- Built lifelong trust—ensured that their bond grew beyond coach-athlete by becoming a mentor and a father figure to Phelps.

That level of intentional one-on-one coaching, focused on both performance and the person, is what transformed a talented swimmer into the greatest Olympian of all time.

Coaching Session #2: Small Group Coaching

If your team is on the larger side and you can't meet with everyone one-on-one each week, small group coaching might just save the day.

This format allows you to develop key sales skills across a small peer group. Ideally, you want to involve four to six people per session. Sessions typically run an hour or two, but anything longer and you're likely drifting away from microskill development and into training mode.

I often get asked, "When should I use small group coaching?" The answer is all the time.

I recommend getting a handful of your salespeople together at least a couple of times per month to work on revenue-generating skills as a team.

Here's why small group coaching is so powerful:

- Peer Learning: Team members get to hear how others think and apply techniques like overcoming objections, building rapport, and crafting follow-up strategies.
- Increased Engagement: Let's be honest: it's easy to hide in big meetings. Not here. In a small group, everyone has to participate, which means you'll hear from people you don't normally hear from.
- Safe Practice Space: Most people don't love role-playing, but in a small group, it feels safer. There's less pressure and more support. If you're running the session virtually, break the group into pairs and use private breakout rooms for focused skill practice.

Coaching Session #3: Large Group Coaching

Large group coaching typically happens with your entire sales team, either in person or virtually. When I was a sales leader at a company in Phoenix, these sessions became the highlight of our weekly meetings. Instead of sitting through a boring presentation, the team got to engage, participate, and walk away with a real skill they could use immediately.

Ironically, large group coaching is the most common format . . . and also the hardest to run effectively. Why? Because it's easy for people to hide, drift, or even fake participation, especially when you're working on specific behaviors or microskills.

To make large group coaching sessions truly effective, here are four key principles:

1. **Focus on One Microskill.** I know it sounds obvious, but sales leaders often fall into the trap of trying to do too much. The thinking goes, "Well, I've got everyone here; might as well pack in as much as possible." That's a mistake. Too much content overwhelms your team and waters down the impact. Instead, go deep on one skill, like handling a specific objection or crafting a follow-up video.

2. **Make It Interactive.** The more your team engages, the more they'll remember. Use these formats:
   - Group discussions
   - Quick pair-and-share moments
   - Small group role-plays
   - Games or challenges

Your goal isn't to lecture; it's to facilitate practice and peer learning.

3. **Assign Coaching Roles.** If you have a larger team, you'll need help with hands-on coaching during the session.
   - Tap into other managers or team leads who are present.
   - Use peer coaching by breaking into groups of three:
     - One person is the salesperson
     - One is the customer
     - One is the coach, giving feedback after the role-play

This structure multiplies the value of the session without putting it all on your shoulders.

4. **End with a Clear Call to Action.** To ensure real-world application, always wrap the session with a specific task. If you just trained on video follow-up, challenge the team to send one personalized video to a prospect in the next twenty-four hours. Or make it fun: "Whoever sends the most follow-up videos this week wins a prize."

That competitive nudge can drive real behavior change and give you great material to spotlight in your next session.

Summary

Mastery doesn't come from doing everything at once . . . It comes from focusing on one small skill at a time. The best coaches know that real growth happens when you zoom in, not out. It's not about getting better at follow-up; it's about improving the first five seconds of a voicemail. Microskill development is where progress lives. The mistake many sales leaders make is trying to fix everything all at once, which overwhelms the team and leads to almost nothing sticking.

To avoid that trap, great leaders structure their coaching around focused, intentional formats: one-on-one sessions for deep development, small groups for peer learning and practice, and large group coaching for team alignment and momentum. Each session type plays a role, but the secret to effectiveness is the same across the board—narrow the focus, make it interactive, and always end with a clear next step. When a sales leader learns to coach this way, they stop managing from the sidelines and start actively driving performance. They become more than a manager . . . they become a RevenueGetter.

Questions to Ponder

- Do you tend to coach broad outcomes or specific behaviors? Think back to a recent situation . . . Could you have zoomed in on a microskill instead of giving general direction?
- Which coaching format are you using most, and which are you underutilizing? How can you be more intentional with one-on-one, small group, and large group coaching to drive consistent development?
- Are you actively helping your team improve or hoping they figure it out on their own? What would it look like for you to step fully into the role of a RevenueGetter this week?

CHAPTER FOUR

IDENTIFYING THE MICROSKILLS THAT MATTER

In an investigation, details matter.

—Jack Reacher

I got my start in coaching back in the late '90s at a telemarketing firm in Arizona called Direct Marketing Services, DMS for short. I loved it. The rush of closing sales with complete strangers was exhilarating.

One day, while I was on the sales floor, the training manager, Finley Hammond, approached me. Finley was a master trainer. He was extremely sharp, motivational, and always full of energy. He even had a side hustle called Motivational Excellence, where he sold branded clothing with inspirational slogans. I admired Finley a lot.

He pulled me aside and said something that would change the trajectory of my life: "Ryan, you'd make a great trainer. You're quick on your feet, you're funny, and I think you could do it . . . if you're interested."

I was in my early twenties, still figuring out what I wanted to do with my life. So, I asked the most obvious question: "What does it pay?"

Soon after, I found myself stepping into my first training role. And Finley's first assignment for me ended up being a lesson I still teach today. (In fact, I used it just two days before writing this chapter!)

There was a guy on the telemarketing floor named Scott who was absolutely crushing it. He was making $60,000–$70,000 a year . . . as a telemarketer. That kind of money on the phones in the '90s? You were either superhuman or possibly not human at all. Most of the team was averaging closer to $20,000 a year.

Finley came to me and said, "Ryan, I need you to figure out what Scott is doing differently than everyone else."

I started listening to Scott nonstop. At first, I couldn't figure it out. Sure, he was smooth, but he wasn't saying anything radically different. Then I shifted my focus and started listening to the average reps, the $20,000 crowd. That was when it clicked.

I was listening to a rep named Jeff. On his third call, this is what I heard:

Jeff: "Is John there?"

John: "This is him."

Jeff: "Hi John, my name is Jeff, and I'm calling on behalf of US West."

The way Jeff said it, his voice went up at the end of the sentence as if he was asking a question. Then he paused. That pause was all the opening the prospect needed.

John: "Are you sure?" (click)

John slammed the phone down.

That moment was pivotal for me. I realized that Jeff, and likely most of the other reps, were using an up tone that made them sound uncertain, even insecure. Scott, on the other hand, used a down tone. His delivery was confident, controlled, and final.

That was the moment I discovered the power of microskills. I sprinted around the call center, coaching everyone to drop their tone at the right moment. And like magic, results started improving.

As a sales leader, you're not just looking for who's not performing; you're investigating why. Coaching isn't about broad strokes. It's about the subtle things. The small behaviors. The tiny details that, when added up, create meaningful impact.

That's where microskills come in.

So how do you identify which microskills need coaching? The key is to gather insights from multiple sources to get a clear picture of where the performance gaps are. The following are a few specific methods you can use to uncover the information needed to pinpoint exactly what to coach each salesperson on.

Method #1: Direct Observation

A few years ago, I was working with a new home sales team in Southern California. Their VP of sales, Peter, invited me out on a Saturday to help work the floor and observe the team in action.

The team had about four salespeople and one greeter. It was a mix of seasoned veterans and newer faces. Peter and I started the day by assisting a couple who wanted to tour the models. After we wrapped up with them, I noticed one of the salespeople, Parker, was nowhere to be found. He had vanished for about an hour, so I went looking for him.

The sales office was a sprawling welcome center. It's exactly what you'd expect from a 55+ community trying to paint the picture of retirement living at its finest. After a bit of searching, I found Parker tucked away in the most remote office in the building. The office had glass walls and was in the back corner. It was practically hidden. Inside, Parker was sitting with a couple and what looked like their Realtor.

Now, Parker was brand-new to new home sales. Mid-twenties, clean-cut, and just about the nicest guy you could meet. But what really caught my attention? He was sweating. A lot. The couple seemed to be running the conversation, and Parker looked overwhelmed. I finally caught Parker's attention and motioned for him to step outside.

The moment he walked out, he said, "Thank you so much. This couple is killing me!"

I asked what was going on, and he told me, "This is their twelfth visit. They just won't pull the trigger."

So, I asked a simple question that revealed the real issue: "Have you asked them to buy?"

He stared at me like I had three heads. After a pause, he said, "Well, no. I don't think they're ready."

That right there was the problem.

With that piece of intel, I gave Parker clear direction on what to do with the prospects. I said, "Okay . . . Go back in there and give them a gift. Tell them today is the day they get the gift of decision. Let them know you're going to leave them alone to decide, yes or no. Either answer is fine. But today is their last visit."

Parker looked terrified. And that was when I realized the microskill he was missing: **confidence**. His voice, body language, and hesitation all pointed to someone who was hoping the buyer would close themselves.

To his credit, Parker went back in and did exactly what I coached him to do.

The result? The couple bought that day.

Parker kept building on that lesson. He started asking for the sale, early and often. Today, he's a sales leader at one of the fastest-growing home builders in the country.

What's the takeaway?

You can't see everything from the CRM, a pipeline review call, or a team meeting. Some of the most valuable performance gaps only show up when you observe in the field, including the following:

- Confidence issues in tone, body language, or word choice
- Salespeople who dive into financials too early
- Weak or passive objection handling

There are two powerful ways to get this kind of direct observation:

1. **Shadowing:** Sit with your salesperson and observe how they work in real time.
2. **Mystery Shopping:** If your industry allows it, mystery shops can be incredibly valuable. Yes, some reps can spot a shopper, but the insights are still worth it. I always remember the old saying "How you do anything is how you do everything."

Direct observation is the single most effective way to uncover performance gaps and identify the microskills your team needs to improve. Ironically, it's also the thing most sales leaders do the least. In chapter 14, we'll talk about time blocking and how corporate meetings often crowd out this high-impact activity.

But for now, just remember, if you want to be a true RevenueGetter, you've got to get out in the field and observe!

Method #2: Role-Play Exercises

Building on the phrase "How you do anything is how you do everything," role-plays are a great tool for uncovering performance gaps.

I know the average salesperson doesn't exactly enjoy role-play. It's uncomfortable and shines a light on where the performance gaps are . . . and that's the point. I'm a big fan of partnering salespeople up and having them practice with each other. The more they role-play, the more comfortable, and ultimately more skilled, they become. The key here is I don't make them look stupid in front of the team. I tend to have them partner up and practice in an environment where they feel safe to fail.

Back in 2016, I was coaching a salesperson named Derek. Derek was the kind of guy everyone liked. He was humble, laid-back, and just cool to be around.

That is . . . until it was time to ask for the sale.

During a role-play session focused on closing, Derek suddenly transformed from smooth to strange. At the moment he was supposed to go in for the close, he extended both hands out in front of him as if he was about to strangle someone and said, in a slow, almost eerie tone: "Do you want to take it off the market?"

It was bizarre. As I like to say in my keynotes:

Don't be a weirdo.

That one move completely changed the vibe. He went from cool to completely awkward. His sales partner even chimed in and said, "Yeah . . . you do that all the time."

That's the beauty of role-play. It exposes the weird stuff salespeople don't even realize they're doing.

I spent the next twenty minutes working with Derek on how to ask for the sale in a way that felt natural and confident. No jazz hands. No horror-movie energy. Just calm, casual clarity.

The following week, Derek sold four homes. #Boom.

I'll go deeper into how I coached Derek in Chapter 9, but for now, just recognize that role-plays give you a front-row seat to the microskills that need attention. And when you're watching closely, you'll start to see things in practice that you might have missed in the field.

And if you start to notice the same performance gaps popping up across multiple people? That's your cue to bring it into a group coaching session or your next sales meeting.

Salespeople need practice. Coaches need visibility. Role-plays deliver both.

Method #3: Performance Data Analysis

I'll be honest; I'm not a huge fan of most sales reports. They rarely tell you much about microskill gaps. That said, there are a few key data points that can help you spot where to focus your coaching efforts. Here are three to pay attention to:

- **CRM Activity (Customer Relationship Manager)**

Reviewing your team's CRM entries can give you a window into both effort and quality. Look at follow-up frequency, timing, and especially the quality of the notes. I'm not just looking for facts . . . I'm looking for stories.

Notes that include a buyer's emotional drivers ("they want to be closer to their grandkids") tell me the salesperson is digging deeper. I want to see the *why*, not just the *what*. Surface-level notes like "looking for low payment" or "really liked the Tarrington product" aren't enough.

- **Customer Feedback**

If your company uses surveys, you've got a gold mine of insight. Feedback, positive or negative, can quickly reveal where your team is thriving or struggling. If surveys aren't part of your process, pick up the phone and call buyers directly. Ask about their experience. Online reviews can also be a source of coaching insight if you're paying close attention. The key here is to look for patterns.

- **Conversion Ratios**

This is one of the most telling metrics you have. It's not just about how many sales someone is making; it's about how well they're moving people through the process. Look at ratios like these:

- Traffic-to-appointment
- Appointment-to-write
- Write-to-close

When someone has high traffic but low conversions, that's usually a red flag for a microskill breakdown. Maybe they're struggling with rapport, asking for the sale, handling objections, or uncovering needs.

Low traffic but high conversions might mean they're strong in the sales process but weak in prospecting or follow-up. Or you might have a traffic-reporting issue on your hands.

Conversion ratios are like a breadcrumb trail. They don't tell you exactly what's wrong, but they point you to where to start looking.

Method #4: Pipeline Impact Calls

As a sales leader, you'll often find yourself strategizing with your team on how to convert leads that are right on the edge but for some reason just aren't crossing the finish line. At their core, these conversations are about one thing: improving conversion.

During these pipeline impact calls, you'll ask targeted questions to dig into the status of a lead. For example, you might ask:

- What problem are we trying to solve for the customer?
- How did the presentation end?
- When is the next appointment, and what's your follow-up plan?
- What objections came up, and how did you handle them?

These questions are designed to do more than check in—they give you insight into the real performance gaps in your salesperson's process.

Let's say you ask, "How did the presentation end?" and your salesperson responds, "They just started looking, so they weren't ready."

That's a red flag.

Chances are high that you've uncovered a closing skill gap . . . especially if you hear that same excuse more than once across your team.

Patterns like this tell you where to focus your coaching. These aren't just lead reviews; they're diagnostic tools. When used consistently, they'll reveal which microskills are missing and give you the direction you need to improve your team's conversion rate.

Method #5: AI Performance Monitoring

In recent years, several companies have introduced technology designed to record and analyze your sales team's customer interactions. Here's how it works: Your team simply opens an app on their phone, presses record, and the system captures the conversation.

You might be thinking, "Can't we already do that?" The answer is yes . . . and no. Traditional recording tools capture the audio, but these new AI-powered platforms go far beyond that. They can also do the following:

- Summarize the visit
- Measure the conversation against your specific training program
- Pinpoint performance gaps
- Recommend ways to close those gaps

While still relatively new and being tested in the field, AI performance monitoring shows promise as an intel-gathering tool for coaches. There are pros and cons to consider, and its long-term effectiveness is yet to be proven. My bet? This technology will only get more refined and more valuable as its popularity grows.

Summary

Great sales performance doesn't hinge on charisma or direction from a manager in a sales meeting; it comes from mastering the microskills. These are the small, often invisible behaviors that separate average salespeople from top performers: tone of voice, body language, timing, phrasing, and emotional awareness. As a sales leader, your job isn't just to notice *who* is struggling but to uncover *why*. That requires a detective's mindset. You need to pay close attention to subtle cues and coach the precise behaviors that move the needle.

You can't coach what you can't see. That's why visibility is everything. Whether through direct observation, role-plays, customer feedback, conversion data, or strategic lead conversations, the more ways you watch your salespeople work, the clearer the performance picture becomes. When you consistently zoom in on microskills, you will do more than improve your team's conversion efforts; you will build confident, consistent professionals who know how to close with intention and authenticity.

Questions to Ponder

- Where in your team's sales process might microskills be breaking down without you realizing it?
- Do you have a system in place to consistently observe and identify these subtle performance gaps?
- What one microskill, if improved across the team, would have the biggest impact on revenue?

CHAPTER FIVE

BUILDING A CULTURE OF COACHING

Culture eats strategy for breakfast.

—Peter Drucker

Hilti Corporation, a global leader in construction tools and services, recognized the need to evolve its organizational culture to maintain a competitive edge. Historically, while Hilti's managers excelled in technical expertise, there was a gap in consistent coaching and employee development practices. Coaching was often sporadic and primarily directed at underperforming employees, leaving a significant portion of the workforce without structured developmental support.

To address this, Hilti launched a comprehensive coaching and mentoring program aimed at transforming those in managerial roles from mere supervisors to proactive coaches. This initiative included these key components:

- **Structured Training Programs:** Since 2010, Hilti has implemented regular ILM (Institute of Leadership and Management) Coaching and Mentoring training sessions across its global locations. These programs were tailored to accommodate the diverse linguistic and cultural backgrounds of its employees, ensuring effective communication and understanding.

- **Integration of Coaching into Daily Operations:** The company emphasized the importance of embedding coaching conversations into routine managerial practices. This approach aimed to make coaching a natural and expected aspect of the employee experience rather than an isolated activity.
- **Utilization of External Expertise:** Hilti collaborated with organizations like InsideOut Development to equip their managers with effective coaching models and tools. This partnership focused on enhancing the quality of performance-management conversations and fostering a culture where employees felt engaged and supported.

Hilti's deliberate move to embed coaching into its corporate culture highlights the profound impact that structured employee development can have on both individual and organizational performance. By prioritizing coaching, Hilti not only enhanced its internal culture but also solidified its position in the competitive construction sector.

The Coaching Culture Difference

It's probably no surprise that Hilti saw significant improvements in their culture and their revenue. In fact, when you create a culture of coaching, everything arguably improves. Here are just a few examples that Hilti, and many other organizations, tend to see:*

* "Case Study: Hilti Corporation," Coaching Culture at Work/Culture at Work, https://www.coachingcultureatwork.com/case-studies-coaching-programmes/coaching-mentoring-training-switzerland/.

- Happier employees
- Higher team engagement
- Improved customer service
- Increased production output
- Increased revenue

The Hiring Dilemma

When I'm conducting a sales seminar, I often ask the sales leader, in front of the team, if they've ever had the "perfect" résumé land on their desk. You know the one . . . all the accolades, all the awards. It's like the clouds parted and God gifted you the salesperson who's going to save the company . . . and your job.

Then I ask that sales leader if they've ever brought that same person into an interview and, within thirty seconds or so, thought to themselves, "Uhhhh . . . how about no!"

Every sales leader laughs and says, "Absolutely."

That response tells me one thing: Sales leaders are looking for more than just sales skills. The real question is, What are they looking for? Sure, "culture fit" comes to mind, but that's often too vague to be useful.

For me, it comes down to two critical traits every sales leader should hire for:

1. **Coachability**
2. **Drive**

If you bring someone on board who isn't coachable, you get what you get. There's little chance of leveling them up. And heaven help you if you change your sales strategy or, God forbid, upgrade your CRM. Expect pushback.

Here's the other thing about uncoachable people: They're often riddled with pride.

Years ago, I was in Austin, Texas, running a performance improvement training with a new home sales team. The managers and I were doing one-on-one coaching throughout the session. One of the coaches, Chelsea, approached a salesperson I will call Nick.

Now, picture a walking Texas cliché: big belt buckle, thick mustache, boots, and jeans that would make a schoolgirl blush. That was Nick.

Chelsea, fresh off the sales floor and eager to coach, walked into the role-play area where Nick and his partner were "practicing" (insert sarcasm). After watching him handle an objection, Chelsea offered some praise and a tip for improvement. Nick, who had apparently been selling longer than Chelsea had been alive, looked her dead in the eye and said, in the most condescending tone possible: "Sweetheart, I've been doing this for thirty years. I know what I'm doing."

Chelsea paused, likely shocked by Nick's offensive statement, then smiled and replied, "Wow. That's amazing. Do it again."

Nick was the furthest thing from coachable. Honestly, I don't think he had thirty years of experience. I think he had one year of experience, repeated thirty times in a row.

And here's the truth: You can't train coachability. Believe me, I've tried.

My mom was a severe alcoholic. I remember trying over and over to help her change. I learned the hard way that coachability has to come from within. I learned that lesson when I was just eleven.

One Saturday, I decided my mom was going to get sober. While she was passed out, I gathered every bottle of Smirnoff, every can of Budweiser . . . everything she had, and dumped it all down the sink.

Quick question—what do you think happened when she woke up?

Let's just say I learned a tough lesson that day: You can't force someone to change. They have to want it.

Same goes for your sales team. It's easier to hire someone who's eager to grow than to try to convince a Nick to evolve.

Now let's talk about drive. Same principle. Motivation is an inside job. That's why motivational seminars wear off after a few days. You're better off hiring someone who's hungry to win.

Back in 2004, our leadership team was conducting a group interview with six candidates. One of them was a twenty-two-year-old named Brandon. He had zero experience and didn't exactly wow us in the interview, so he got the polite "thanks but no thanks" letter.

A few days later, a package showed up at our corporate office . . . from Brandon.

Now, we didn't usually get packages from candidates we'd already turned down (in fact, we never did), so we were hesitant to open it. This was also during the anthrax scare, so naturally, everyone was like, "You open it"—"No, you open it."

Eventually, I opened it.

Inside was a single tennis shoe and a rolled-up sheet of paper tied with a ribbon. The note read:

Just trying to get my foot in the door.
Give me a shot, and I won't let you down.

Of course, we called him. And we hired him.

Brandon was so excited. And because of his hunger to succeed and his coachability, we placed him in one of our toughest selling opportunities, where no one could seem to sell a home.

Brandon went in and dominated. He outworked and outlearned everyone else who had tried to succeed there.

Hire for coachability and drive, and your life as a leader will get a whole lot easier, especially when it comes to coaching for performance improvement.

Who Gets Coaching? Everyone

I once worked with a sales leader named Ben. At first glance, he seemed like the gold standard. He was inspiring and supportive. His top performers sang his praises and swore he was the best boss they'd ever had. If you only looked at the results and morale of the top half of his team, you'd think Ben was crushing it.

Then, seemingly out of nowhere, a lawsuit hit against our company—specifically against Ben.

The charge? Favoritism and wrongful termination.

As the facts came to light, the issue became clear: Ben was doing a fantastic job with the people he liked. If you were part of his inner circle, you got attention, coaching, encouragement, and opportunity.

But if you weren't . . . if you were new, quiet, or just didn't "click," you were overlooked. No coaching. No development. No chance to grow.

Ben's mistake wasn't that he coached people. His mistake was who he chose to coach and who he left behind.

Assuming you have a team of coachable salespeople, there are still traps that can sabotage your coaching culture. The biggest? Believing that some people don't need or deserve coaching.

If your goal is a true coaching culture, there's only one answer to the question "Who gets coaching?"

Everyone.

That doesn't mean equal time for all. It means intentional time for all. Let's break it down.

The Four Categories of Salespeople

1. **Stars:** These are your top performers. They manage their business well, deliver results, and often cover

sales gaps. They're self-sufficient, but they still need development to avoid complacency or burnout.

2. **Climbers:** High-potential, hungry team members working their way into the top tier. They ask for help often and benefit greatly from feedback. Invest in their momentum.
3. **Coasters:** Consistent but stagnant. They fly under the radar and often get ignored. This group needs coaching to break habits of mediocrity and reignite ambition.
4. **Strugglers:** Bottom performers. They usually receive the most coaching, but that coaching must be strategic, time bound, and paired with clear expectations.

Although the numbers can vary based on several factors, a typical sales organization tends to break down into the following percentages per category:

- Stars—20 percent
- Climbers—30 percent
- Coasters—30 percent
- Strugglers—20 percent

Understanding this distribution allows you to be more intentional with your time. You may not coach each group exactly the same way, but if you're not coaching one or more of the groups at all, you're leaving revenue and growth on the table.

Summary

Coaching isn't just an activity—it's a mindset. Companies like Hilti have proven that when coaching is embedded into the culture, both people and profits rise. But culture doesn't just happen. It's shaped by the choices leaders make about who they invest in and how often.

If you want to build a culture of coaching, start by hiring the right people. Look for people with drive and coachability. Then, commit to coaching everyone. You don't need to coach everyone equally, but you do need to coach everyone intentionally. Stars, Climbers, Coasters, and Strugglers all deserve to be developed. If you only coach the few, you send a silent message to the rest: You don't matter. And that's how potential gets wasted. True leaders coach the whole team.

Questions to Ponder

- Which category do most of your current coaching efforts fall into, and who might be getting overlooked as a result?
- What systems or habits can you implement to ensure that every salesperson on your team receives meaningful development, regardless of performance level?
- If someone shadowed your coaching interactions for thirty days, what would they say your coaching culture actually looks like?

CHAPTER SIX

WHO IS THE COACHING FOR ANYWAY?

You do not motivate people.
You uncover what motivates them and help them reach it.

—Ken Blanchard

In late 2015, I received a call from a VP of sales named Patrick. Clearly very frustrated, Patrick said, "I've got to ask you a question. How do you handle a top producer who doesn't want any coaching?" This is a fairly common question, and I was stoked that Patrick was asking. Most sales leaders just stop trying to coach the top performer and turn into the sales leader we called the Ghost in chapter 2.

Here is how the rest of the conversation went:

Ryan: "Tell me what happened . . . There's got to be a story here."

Patrick: "Well, I got this guy on my team named Mike. He's been the top producer forever, but I feel like he could do even better. The challenge is he is totally turned off to any coaching I try to give him."

Ryan: "OK . . . so what happened most recently that has you calling me?"

Patrick: "Well, I scheduled a coaching session with Mike, and when we got into the coaching, it was obvious he didn't want to do it. But this time, he interrupted me and said, 'Why are you trying to coach me? I am your best salesperson, and I know what I'm doing. Why don't you go help someone who isn't selling?' Honestly, Ryan, it threw me for a loop because he's never flat out said it to my face. My question is, How do I get that guy to perform at an even higher level?"

Ryan: "Wow. Can I ask you a few questions about the coaching itself before I answer that?"

Patrick: "Sure."

Ryan: "You said you scheduled the coaching. Can I ask what the meeting was called on your calendar?"

Patrick: "The B-lead conversion meeting."

Ryan: "Okay . . . based on the title alone, who is the session for, Mike or you?"

Patrick: "I guess me."

Ryan: "You're right. And in order to coach anyone properly, you have to make the coaching be about helping them get what they want . . . not what you want."

It's not about you

Patrick went on to ask me how that could be accomplished. I gave him an assignment to take Mike out to coffee and get to know him. No business. No conversion conversations and definitely no coaching. Just get to know the guy and see if Mike had any reason to get better at selling. Were there any gaps in Mike's life that Patrick could help with?

The following week, Patrick texted me and asked if I could chat really quick. I could tell by his tone that something likely happened with Mike. With similar excitement, I asked, "All right, what happened with Mike?"

Patrick replied, "I did exactly what you said. At first the coffee was kind of awkward, but as soon as Mike realized I wasn't going to jam coaching down his throat and that he wasn't being fired, he started to open up."

I asked, "What did you learn about him?" The anticipation was killing me.

Patrick said, "Apparently, no one in Mike's family has gone to college, including him. He has two daughters, and he has a goal to send both of them to college, 100 percent paid for. The challenge is that because of the downturn in 2008, he is about $60,000 off of being able to achieve that goal for his youngest daughter, Jessica."

Let me pause the story here to ask you, the reader, a question. If you were Patrick, what would you name the next coaching session with Mike?

I asked Patrick the same question, and he said, "This will now be called 'Jessica's college fund session.'"

Sure enough, Patrick was able to get through to Mike to improve Mike's selling skills. And because the coaching sessions shifted from being for Patrick and the company to Mike and his mission, the coaching was received and implemented. Ultimately, the lesson here for every sales leader is that it's not about you.

Uncover Their Why

The reality is simple: People do what's in *their* best interests, not yours. That means coaching, like sales, is ultimately about understanding motivation.

In my sales-training seminars, I often teach that the best kind of urgency is the buyer's urgency. In other words, if you want to sell effectively, uncover why the buyer wants what you're offering and how your product will improve their life. Coaching works the same way. You need to uncover why the salesperson wants coaching in the first place.

Unfortunately, many sales leaders fall into a lazy assumption: that all salespeople are motivated by money. Yes, people like money. But it's rarely the core reason they change behavior, build new skills, or sustain high performance.

So what do most leaders do? They run a sales contest. But here's the problem: Only a small slice of the team usually responds to monetary contests. Assuming cash is the *only* motivator is like assuming your spouse only feels loved when you take them out to dinner. It's shallow, limited, and often misses the point.

In his book *Drive*, Daniel Pink cites MIT research showing that when a task requires even basic cognitive skill, external rewards like money actually reduce performance.[*] In sales, where emotional intelligence, judgment, and timing matter most, that's a wake-up call. If you want better performance, you need to tap into the salesperson's internal drive, not just their paycheck.

The Five Sales Motivators

In his best-selling book, *The Five Love Languages*, author Dr. Gary Chapman reveals that humans give and receive love very

---

* Daniel H. Pink, *Drive: The Surprising Truth About What Motivates Us* (Riverhead Books, 2011).

differently.* Some know they are loved through receiving gifts. Others achieve that same feeling by spending quality time with their partner. And others use acts of service as the measure.

The motivation of a salesperson is very similar. Some like gifts, while others like quality time or praise. Look at the list below and think about specific team members you manage. Do any of these motivators jump off the page for specific individuals?

Motivator	Meaning
Quality Time	This rep is fueled by connection. They want time with family, friends, or even with their leader. Coaching and rewards that allow for more meaningful time off or deeper relationships will drive them.
Praise/ Recognition	They thrive when their effort is seen and appreciated. Public praise, shoutouts in meetings, or a personal note from a leader can go further than a bonus.
Gifts/Money	Tangible rewards motivate them. Cash bonuses, gift cards, or incentive prizes can activate their competitive edge.
Life Balance	They are motivated by flexibility, stress reduction, or time freedom. Extra days off, shift swaps, or a simplified workload have a big impact.
Growth Opportunity	These reps want to improve, advance, and be challenged. What fuels them is skill-building, stretch assignments, or the next leadership step.

In 2018, I was working with a sales leader named Angie, who called for some one-on-one coaching. Angie needed to boost sales and

* Gary Chapman, *The Five Love Languages: The Secret to Love That Lasts*, 4th ed. (Northfield Publishing, 2014).

wanted to run a sales contest idea by me. After she got done explaining how the contest would run, I asked, "What are the prizes?"

She replied, "Cold hard cash!"

I paused.

Angie's excitement toned down a little, and then she asked, "Is that wrong?"

I said, "It's not wrong; it's just not what will motivate your *entire* team." I went on to explain the concept that a small percentage of people are truly motivated by money. I asked if I could suggest a reward system that would fire up the entire team rather than a select few.

Of course, Angie replied, "Heck yeah!"

I suggested she sit down with every salesperson and have a conversation about their "why." The goal, much like Patrick's goal at the beginning of the chapter, was to get to know their team and uncover what truly drives them. Angie heard me out and said, "That sounds like a lot of work."

My reply was simple (and stolen from Jim Rohn):

"Don't wish it were easier. Wish you were better."

With that, Angie did exactly what I coached her to do. The rewards she developed were completely based on what motivated each individual. When the contest was over, Angie had hit her goal, but there was one standout story that she had to tell me about. Angie had a salesperson by the name of Dorothy. Dorothy was a veteran salesperson. Not a hotshot but not a bad performer. What was interesting about Dorothy was that she was never at the top of the sales leaderboard. Contests never inspired her or improved Dorothy's performance . . . until this contest.

When Angie sat down to get to know Dorothy's real motivation, she uncovered that Dorothy hadn't had a weekend off in roughly fifteen years. When Angie dug into what issues this might be causing in Dorothy's life, here is what Dorothy told her:

"I have a granddaughter, and we have never spent a full day together. I see her here and there and with the family at holidays, but I really want to have a one-on-one granddaughter day with her."

Can you guess the reward Angie came up with for Dorothy?

Angie told Dorothy that when she hit the stretch goal, she would give her an entire weekend off, and the company would pay for a mani-pedi, lunches and dinners, and a show or movie for her and her granddaughter.

I think you could guess that Dorothy, *for the first time ever*, not only hit the goal; she blew it out of the water! Angie hasn't run a money-only contest since.

Your Assignment

As I did with Angie and have done with countless other sales leaders, I have an assignment for you. Get to know every salesperson on your team. Engage in personal conversations about their lives in order to find out how you can serve them as their leader.

Use the tool at the end of this chapter to capture what you learned about each team member. Then you will review it before every coaching session to make sure that you are framing the coaching as something that is *for* them, not *to* them.

You will need to be extremely curious with your team. You cannot be surface level in your conversation, or you won't uncover the real motivators. Here are a few sample questions that you might ask.

Motivator Discovery Questions

Use these questions during one-on-one conversations to uncover what truly drives each salesperson. These are meant to be open ended, life centered, and curiosity based.

- "What's something big you're working toward in your personal life right now?"
- "If you had an extra $25,000 this year, what would you do with it?"
- "What's a personal goal you've set that you haven't hit yet?"
- "Is there something you'd like to do for your family that feels out of reach right now?"
- "What's one thing that would make your life outside of work easier or more fun?"
- "If we could remove one stressor from your life, what would it be?"
- "What does success look like for you beyond the leaderboard?"
- "What motivates you more: being recognized, being challenged, or having time freedom?"
- "If I could help you achieve one nonwork goal this year, what would you choose?"

Summary

Coaching isn't about getting your team to do what you want; it's about helping them get what they want. Too often, sales leaders try to improve performance through company-driven goals, financial contests, or rigid structures. But real coaching begins when you uncover what motivates each individual. That means slowing down long enough to learn about their lives, their families, their goals, and their personal pain points. When you connect coaching to their mission, whether that's paying for a daughter's college, getting a weekend with a granddaughter, or achieving a personal breakthrough, performance follows naturally.

This chapter is a call to shift your coaching from compliance to connection. Instead of leading with metrics, lead with curiosity. The best sales coaches don't push their team, they pull out the internal motivations. They align company growth with individual purpose. And when that alignment happens, people stop resisting coaching and start asking for it. Why? Because it's no longer about doing more for the company—it's about doing more for their own life.

Questions to Ponder

- When was the last time you uncovered a team member's personal motivation, and did you build your coaching around it?
- How much of your current coaching agenda is based on your needs versus theirs?
- If every coaching session had to be named after your salesperson's goal, what would you call your next one?

CHAPTER SEVEN

THE THREE GOALS OF EVERY COACHING SESSION

Coaching is unlocking a person's potential
to maximize their own performance.
It is helping them to learn rather than teaching them.

—Sir John Whitmore

In the world of personal development, there's a popular story about a Harvard study from the 1930s that tracked graduates and compared their success based on whether they had written goals. The story claims that those with written goals far outperformed their peers over the next thirty years. It's a compelling tale, but there's just one problem: The study never actually happened.

Despite the myth, modern research does back up the core idea. A well-documented study from Gail Matthews at Dominican University in 2007 found that people who wrote down their goals were significantly more likely to achieve them than those who merely thought about their goals.* In fact, participants who wrote down their goals,

* Sarah Gardner and Dave Albee, "Study Focuses on Strategies for Achieving Goals, Resolutions," *Dominican Scholar,* Dominican University of California, February 1, 2015,, https://scholar.dominican.edu/cgi/viewcontent.cgi?article=1265&context=news-releases&utm.

made action commitments, and sent progress reports to a friend were **76 percent more likely to achieve their goals than those who didn't.**

The takeaway? Writing down your goals matters. It brings clarity, focus, and accountability. That applies not only to life goals but also to coaching.

Every coaching session you conduct should have a clear purpose. In this section, I'll walk you through the goals I keep in mind every time I lead a coaching conversation. These aren't necessarily the performance outcomes we're chasing, but they are the behaviors and intentions that drive those results. Adopt one or all of them, and you'll raise the impact of every coaching session you lead.

Goal #1: Master the Framework

When I'm teaching any skill, I lean heavily on frameworks rather than scripts, and for good reason. I firmly believe that today's customers want to connect with a real human, not a sales robot spouting scripted lines they'd never use in a natural conversation.

I've never read a sales script and thought, "Wow . . . this sounds exactly like me!" In fact, try using scripted language on one of your friends and watch how quickly they look at you like you're a weirdo and ask, "What are you doing?" It's awkward, and it kills authenticity.

That's where frameworks come in.

Frameworks give sales professionals structure without stripping them of their personality. They allow reps to stay present in the moment rather than locked into memorization. Take pricing conversations, for example. Price often comes up too early in the sales process. To coach salespeople on how to handle this, I teach them a framework they can make their own instead of scripting a word-for-word response.

Here is that framework:

1. Acknowledge it.
2. Explain it.
3. Defer it.
4. Redirect.
5. Be curious.

If I gave that framework to five different salespeople, you'd hear five totally different responses—*and that's exactly the point.* Frameworks empower salespeople to stay flexible while still hitting the mark. And that leads us to Goal #2 . . .

Goal #2: Find Their Authentic Voice

In the summer of 2014, I was in Southern California leading a coaching session with about eight salespeople. We were practicing how to overcome objections when, during a break, I overheard a conversation between two team members. One of them—let's call her Desiree—was chatting casually and confidently, using expressions like "Girl . . . !" and "I don't play like that."

It was a brief moment, but something about her voice and energy stuck with me.

When we came back from break and began another role-play practice session, I noticed something weird. Desiree sounded completely different. Her tone had changed. Her words were more polished, even stiff. She wasn't showing up as the same person I had just overheard minutes before.

I went up to Desiree and asked her why she sounded totally different. Her response was something I've heard many times: "At work, I try to sound more professional."

Now, I'm all for professionalism, but not when it comes at the cost of authenticity. When salespeople pretend to be someone they're not, it creates distance, not connection. Customers pick up on that. They may not be able to name it, but they can feel it, and it destroys trust.

That's why one of my core coaching goals is to help salespeople find and use their authentic voice. I want them to sound like themselves, not a corporate version of themselves. Because let's be honest: pretending to be someone else all day? That's exhausting.

Now, there is one caveat here. If your "authentic voice" includes cussing like a Quentin Tarantino character, we need to draw a professional line. But outside of that, authenticity is the way to go.

Here are two of the best ways to coach your team into their authentic voice:

1. **Repetition:** When salespeople repeat a framework enough times, it moves from conscious performance to natural expression. That's when their real voice begins to emerge.
2. **Use the Best Friend Test:** If a salesperson sounds stiff or overly polished, ask: "How would you say this to your best friend?" That question almost always unlocks a more relaxed, genuine tone.

Authenticity builds trust. And trust moves the sale forward.

Goal #3: Improve Their Communication Skills

We've all seen that salesperson who checks all the boxes. They ask for the sale, demo the product, and handle objections. But let me ask you this: Have you ever seen a salesperson do all of that while sounding nervous, defensive, or just . . . off?

I have. In fact, I used to be that salesperson.

In 2001, I was selling new homes for a Fortune 100 builder in the Phoenix market. I started off strong. I sold a home on my very first day and wrote fourteen contracts in my first month. I imagine management was wondering what I was doing . . . so they mystery shopped me.

For those unfamiliar, a mystery shop is when a company sends in a fake buyer equipped with a hidden camera to evaluate your sales process. The rest of us, who are familiar with mystery shops? We're rolling our eyes right now (kidding . . . sort of).

One afternoon, a beat-up white Toyota pulled up. An older couple got out and asked specifically for me. My sales partner, Sharma, greeted them first and handed them off. The moment they walked in, the man asked, "Do you have any incentives?"

Let me pause here: I hated that question.

I took a half step back, planted my right foot, and said, "Well, look . . . we do things a little differently here." I had no idea I was being shopped until I was called into the division office to review the footage with my director of sales and sales manager.

They paused the video right at that moment. My manager, Juliet, looked at me and said, "Do you know what this looks like you're about to do?"

I knew. But I shrugged. She said, "It looks like you're about to throw a punch."

And she was right.

Juliet coached me on how to respond to tough questions with calm, open body language. That moment taught me a lesson I've carried ever since: Great salespeople don't just say the right things . . . **they communicate the right way.**

The rest of this chapter explores the three key areas to focus on when coaching your team's communication skills:

1. Words

When coaching salespeople on words, there are two parts to look at:

- Word count
- Word choice

Word Count

Great communicators simplify. They eliminate the fluff. In sales, there's a myth that says, "You're good at sales because you have the gift of gab." Really? I've never walked into a sales office as a customer thinking, "Boy, I hope I get a salesperson who won't shut the heck up."

Too many words cloud your message and confuse your customer. One of the biggest culprits? Asking too many questions at once. Consider these examples:

- Car sales: "Why are you needing a new vehicle? Did you like your old one? Or have you already thought about what you might be interested in?"
- New home sales: "What are you looking for in a home? Have you looked around? Or are you just getting ideas?"
- Insurance: "Are you interested in term? Had a plan before? Or are you thinking whole life?"
- At home: "What do you want for dinner? Italian? Stay in? Are you even hungry?"

Try this instead: Ask *one* clear question and then stop talking. #shutup

Word Choice

I believe some words quietly scream insecurity. Imagine your airline pilot saying, "Hopefully we'll get you there safely." That one word, *hopefully*, destroys confidence.

Coach your team to avoid weak words like these:

- Try
- Hopefully
- Maybe
- Possibly
- Kind of / Sort of

These words signal doubt. Customers don't trust what feels uncertain.

2. Vocal Qualities

Most salespeople speak in a neutral tone and volume, but that's not how emotions are transferred. If you want to influence, your voice has to carry feeling.

One of the best examples I've seen was Zig Ziglar on stage at the Phoenix Suns arena. He was telling a story about his wife, the Redhead, as he called her. When he said her nickname, he whispered it slowly and knelt at the edge of the stage. In response, over twenty thousand people leaned forward. It was the coolest stage moment I have ever witnessed by far.

Start to coach your team to use their voices intentionally. Specifically, focus on these qualities:

- Volume: Project in key moments; soften for intimacy.

- Pitch: Vary tone to hold attention and signal emotion.
- Tonality: Convey warmth, conviction, empathy through tone.
- Speed: Slow down to emphasize; speed up to energize.

3. Body Language

Salespeople often have no idea what their body is communicating. One of the most common issues I see? Salespeople subconsciously shake their heads no when they quote a price or ask for the sale. I'm not suggesting you teach them to nod yes like bobbleheads, but neutral, calm body language creates confidence and connection.

To take this deeper, learn about micro expressions. These are the quick, fleeting facial movements that reveal true emotion. Dr. Paul Ekman, one of *Time* magazine's 100 Most Influential People and a pioneer in this field, defines micro expressions like this:

> *Micro expressions are facial expressions that occur within a fraction of a second. This involuntary emotional leakage exposes a person's true emotions.*[*]

If you want to really nerd out, check out the show *Lie to Me*. It is loosely based on Ekman's work. While dramatized, it's rooted in real science.

Personally, I've had a fascination with body language for as long as I can remember. Growing up with an alcoholic parent, I learned to assess danger from across the room. I could see what kind of night it

---

* Paul Ekman, "Micro Expressions," Paul Ekman Group, accessed September 3, 2025, https://www.paulekman.com/resources/micro-expressions/.

was going to be before I heard a single word. That level of awareness stuck with me, and it's become one of my greatest tools in coaching communication.

When you help your sales team become masters of words, voice, and body language, their confidence grows, their message sharpens, and their results follow.

Summary

Great coaching isn't about winging it. It's about knowing exactly what you're aiming for. Not just the sales numbers you want to hit, but the skills, behaviors, and confidence you want your salespeople to develop. In this chapter, we zeroed in on three coaching goals that make the biggest impact: helping your team master frameworks, speaking with their authentic voice, and elevating their communication skills. Frameworks give structure without turning people into robots; authenticity builds trust; and strong communication, through words, tone, and body language, transforms average performers into credible, confident pros buyers actually want to work with.

When you coach with these goals in mind, you're not simply correcting behavior. You're building capability. You're shaping salespeople who connect with buyers, lead with purpose, and guide people toward decisions that feel right for them. That's the essence of being a RevenueGetter: someone who coaches for connection, leads with intention, and drives results by growing people, not just performance.

Questions to Ponder

- Do your coaching conversations allow room for the salesperson's personality to come through, or are you unintentionally shaping them into a script reader?

- What words, vocal habits, or body language patterns might be quietly undermining your team's credibility with buyers?
- How can you consistently reinforce these three coaching goals in your daily interactions, not just during formal sessions?

CHAPTER EIGHT

THE 4E COACHING METHOD: EXPLAIN

Clarity is the precondition to execution.

—James Clear

As I've mentioned in earlier chapters, most training isn't actually training, and most coaching sessions don't truly qualify as coaching. In both cases, what's happening is usually just a transfer of information. That's not necessarily bad, but it's not coaching. Coaching is about building real skills through intentional development, not simply sharing knowledge.

Over the past twenty-one years, I've used a four-step framework in every coaching session I've led. I call it the 4E Coaching Method™, and it's simple, powerful, and proven. The four steps are as follows:

1. Explain
2. Exhibit
3. Execute
4. Evaluate

In this chapter, we'll explore the first step, *Explain*, and lay the foundation for the coaching process. The next three chapters will walk you through the remaining steps, equipping you with a complete, practical system to coach your salespeople toward lasting growth.

Why Explaining Comes First

Before someone can do something differently, they need to understand *what* they're doing wrong and *why* it matters. That's where most coaching falls apart like a two-dollar suitcase. Sales leaders often assume their team knows what to fix, or they offer vague advice like "build better rapport" or "be more confident." The salesperson nods, walks away, and nothing changes.

Explain is where clarity begins.

This step is all about using clear, direct, and respectful language to describe the gap between current behavior and ideal performance. It's the difference between "You need to improve" and "Let me share with you what happened and what I want it to look like instead."

When done right, Explain activates one of the most powerful learning tools we have: our ability to process and internalize language.

The Power of Auditory Learning

Humans learn in a variety of ways. Primarily, we learn through visual, auditory, and kinesthetic channels. While no one learns exclusively through one style, most people have a dominant preference. According to the VARK learning model developed by Neil Fleming, about 26 percent of people are primarily auditory learners.[*] These individuals

---

* Alina-Mihaela Buşan, "Learning Styles of Medical Students," *Current Health Sciences Journal* 40, no. 2 (March 29, 2014), https://pmc.ncbi.nlm.nih.gov/articles/PMC4340450/.

retain information best through listening, whether it's a conversation, a podcast, or verbal instructions.

But even if your salesperson isn't an auditory learner by default, spoken explanation still plays a key role in understanding. A study conducted by the University of Iowa found that people remember about 20 percent of what they hear, but when verbal communication is paired with other methods (like visual modeling or hands-on practice), retention can jump to over 50 percent.*

What that means for you as a coach is simple: If you don't clearly say *what* needs to change and *why*, you're leaving learning up to chance.

The Formula for Explaining Well

Here's a straightforward method I use to guide the Explain phase in any coaching session. It has three parts:

1. Describe what you observed.
2. Explain why it matters.
3. Define what success looks like.

Let's break that down with an example.

Let's say you're managing a new-home sales team, and you observe a salesperson launching into a new-home tour without asking any questions about the buyer's needs.

---

* Amy Mattson, "In One Ear and Out the Other: Psychology Study Examines How Brains Process and Recall Sounds," Iowa Now, February 26, 2014, https://now.uiowa.edu/news/2014/02/one-ear-and-out-other.

Step 1: Describe what you observed
"In that last conversation, you began walking the buyer through the kitchen before asking any questions about their situation or what they were hoping to find."

Step 2: Explain why it matters
"That makes it feel like they're just part of your routine, rather than you being part of their journey. Buyers want to feel like the home is being chosen with them in mind, not like you're giving a tour to just anyone."

Step 3: Define what success looks like
"Instead, I'd like to see you start with two or three discovery questions before showing anything. Something like: 'What's prompting the move?' or 'What's your vision for your next home?' That small shift helps create an emotional connection and builds trust."

This formula works because it removes ambiguity. To be clear, you're not criticizing; you're clarifying. And most importantly, you're giving the person you're coaching a clear target to aim for next time.

Why Vague Coaching Fails

Let's take a look at some of the most common phrases sales managers use when coaching. These types of phrases almost never lead to change:

- "You need to step up your energy." (What does that even look like?)
- "Try to connect better with the buyer." (Try????)

- "Be more confident." (Uhhh . . . okay.)
- "You need to do a better job closing." (Again . . . what does that look like?)

These all sound helpful on the surface, but none of them give the salesperson something specific to do. Instead, effective coaching turns vague suggestions into behavioral instructions:

Instead of "step up your energy," say:

**"When the buyer walked in,
you stayed seated and gave a small wave.
I want you to stand up, smile,
and greet them within three seconds of seeing them."**

Instead of "connect better," say:

**"You asked three closed-ended questions in a row.
Let's switch one of those to an open-ended question like
'What would make this home feel like yours?'"**

By replacing abstraction with defined action, you move away from vague suggestion to clear strategy.

Explain Is Also About Alignment

Sometimes, leaders hesitate to point out what went wrong because they don't want to discourage or offend their team. But when you avoid explaining what didn't work, you do more damage than good. You leave the person uncertain, and worse—you miss the chance to create alignment.

Think of Explain as your opportunity to say this:

**"We're in this together.
Let me show you where the gap is so we can close it."**

It's not about being critical; it's about being constructive. Great coaching isn't soft or wishy-washy. It's clear. And clarity creates alignment and builds trust.

Applying the Explain Step to the Three Goals of Every Coaching Session

In the last chapter, we discussed the three goals of every coaching session:

1. Master the Framework
2. Find Their Authentic Voice
3. Improve Their Communication Skills

These three goals guide every coaching conversation I have with salespeople. Depending on the specific microskill I'm focused on, I might apply the full 4E Coaching Method to all three goals, or just to one or two. It just depends on whichever goal best supports the behavior we're trying to improve.

Let's say you're observing a salesperson in action—whether it's during a live interaction, a video shop, or a role-play—and they're selling a twelve-week coaching program. The client asks about the price, and the salesperson answers, "That's a good question . . . it's $1,200?" (said with an upward pitch at the end).

That slight upward pitch at the end, as though they're unsure or asking a question, is subtle but powerful. In this situation, we're not coaching them on the price itself. We're coaching them on *vocal quality*, which directly impacts **Goal #3: Improve Communication Skills.**

Here is how a sales leader uses part one of the 4E Coaching Method, Explain:

> **Sales Leader:** "Let's talk about what happened when you shared the price."
>
> **What was observed + why it matters:**
> "You gave the correct number, and I noticed the tone of your voice went up at the end. It came across like a question instead of a confident statement. That one vocal habit can change how the entire message is received. When we sound unsure, even slightly, the buyer starts to question whether they should be confident in us or in the price. We could have had the best presentation up to that point, but the uncertainty in our voice creates doubt.
>
> "What we say is important, but how we say it carries just as much weight, especially when it comes to price."
>
> **Here's what success looks like:**
> "I'd like you to drop the tone at the end of the sentence, so it lands more like a fact or a confident statement rather than a question. Does that make sense to you?"

As I mentioned, you might have to coach your salesperson on how they missed a step of a framework or how they spoke like a robot and need to find their authentic voice. No matter what microskill you are coaching them to improve, all of them have the exact same starting point, explaining what was observed, why it matters, and what success looks like.

Summary

The Explain step of the 4E Coaching Method is where meaningful coaching begins. Without a clear understanding of what went wrong and why it matters, a salesperson is left to guess, repeat old habits, or misinterpret feedback. This chapter outlined a simple but powerful structure for the Explain phase: Describe what was observed, explain why it matters, and define what success looks like. Whether you're addressing a missed behavior in a role-play or a real-time moment from a sales interaction, using this structure ensures clarity, direction, and alignment between you and your salesperson.

Perhaps most importantly, Explain reinforces that coaching is not about criticism; it's about clarity. When done well, it builds trust by showing that you're invested in the salesperson's growth. From vocal tone to body language to behavioral habits, everything improves faster when the gap is identified and understood. Whether you're focused on mastering a framework, helping someone find their authentic voice, or sharpening their communication skills, the first and most vital move is to explain it well.

Questions to Ponder

- Do you tend to give quick fixes or directives during coaching, or do you take the time to truly uncover and articulate the root behavior that needs to change?
- When you explain what went wrong, are you clearly connecting it to why it matters to the buyer, to the outcome, and to the salesperson's growth?
- How often do you turn vague advice into specific, actionable language that gives your salespeople a clear next step?

CHAPTER NINE

THE 4E COACHING METHOD: EXHIBIT

The eye is the gateway to understanding.

—Leonardo da Vinci

In the fall of 2023, my wife, Melissa, and I finally crossed a dream trip off our bucket list: Italy. Ever since we got married in 2010, we'd talked about going, but as anyone who's been knows, two weeks isn't nearly enough to see it all.

We wanted to make the most of every minute. So we asked friends for tips. The responses ranged wildly, from "You need a month just for Rome" to "You can't miss Cinque Terre," which only left us more overwhelmed.

So we turned to the internet's most trusted voice in European travel: Rick Steves. His YouTube videos became our nightly ritual. Each episode didn't just describe what to do . . . he *showed* us. From train stations to street markets, he made it all feel doable. When we found a video that explained how to get from Milan's airport to the train bound for Florence—step by step—we watched it closely.

I was personally really nervous about navigating the transportation routes in Italy, as I had heard some horror stories. When I saw the step-by-step videos on exactly where to go, my confidence skyrocketed.

By the time we landed in Milan, it felt like we had already been there. We walked confidently from customs to the train platform like seasoned travelers. From there, we explored Florence, then Sorrento and the Amalfi Coast, and wrapped up our trip in Rome.

Why did it feel so effortless? Because someone didn't just tell us what to do; they showed us.

The Power of Visual Learning

Visual learning isn't just a learning style preference; it's a proven accelerator for comprehension and retention. Decades of research show that when learners engage with visual elements alongside verbal instruction, their ability to grasp and remember information increases dramatically.

One of the most recognized models illustrating this concept comes from Edgar Dale, who developed the Cone of Learning, also known as the Cone of Experience, in 1946. Dale's model suggests that the way we engage with information directly impacts how well we retain it. For instance, if someone simply hears information (as in the Explain step from the previous chapter), they're likely to retain only about 20 percent of what they learn. But when they both hear the explanation and see it in action (Explain and Exhibit), retention jumps to around 50 percent.

Dale wasn't the first to point out that increased involvement in the learning process boosts retention, but his model remains one of the most widely referenced frameworks for illustrating that truth.

Here's a visual representation of Dale's Cone of Learning:*

---

* Rutvik Thite, "The Cone of Learning," Medium, July 27, 2024, https://medium.com/@rutvikthite17/the-cone-of-learning-3745a81bc6f3.

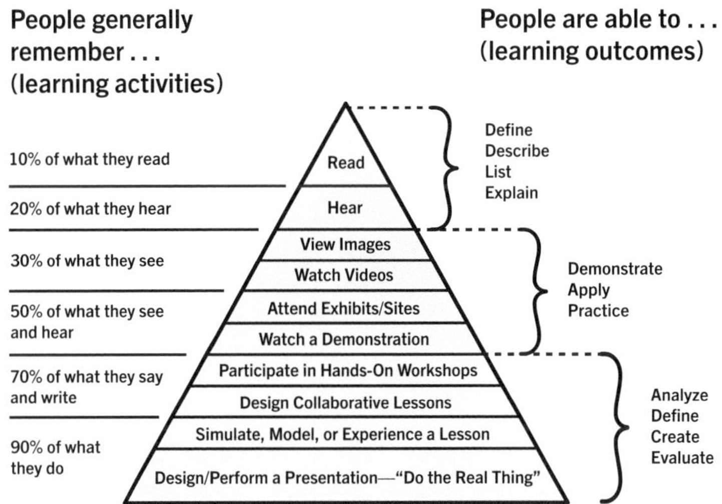

Building on Edgar Dale's Cone of Learning, modern research continues to confirm what great coaches and trainers have known for years: Visual learning makes a major impact.

One well-known study by 3M Corporation and the University of Minnesota found that presentations using visual aids were 43 percent more persuasive than the same presentations without them.* That's a massive lift in effectiveness, simply by adding visuals. When people can *see* what you're saying, they connect more quickly and remember more clearly.

The human brain is wired for visuals. That's why a diagram, photo, or quick sketch can communicate an idea in seconds when words might take minutes.

And when it comes to memory . . . visuals win again. Studies show that after just three days, people remember only 10–20 percent of

* Kat Sikorski, "Visuals Are the Messages in Effective Communications," *Minnesota Cities*, July/August 2023, 28, https://www.qgdigitalpublishing.com/publication/?i=795988&p=0&view=issueViewer.

written or spoken information. But when that same information is paired with visuals, retention jumps to 65 percent.[*] This is called the picture superiority effect.

Here is Wordtracker.com's definition of the picture superiority effect:

> "The picture superiority effect refers to the phenomenon where people remember pictures better than they remember the corresponding words. In other words, pictures are superior over words when it comes to recalling and recognizing information."[†]

Some research even shows that visuals can improve learning by up to 400 percent.[‡] Four. Hundred. Percent. That's not a small boost; it's the difference between someone remembering your coaching and forgetting you were even talking to them!

Visuals also engage. They spark emotion. They bring energy into the conversation. And in coaching, that's critical. When you *Exhibit* a behavior and demonstrate what good looks like, you give your salesperson a picture they can replay, practice, and replicate. That's how transformation happens. Not by just telling. But by showing.

---

* Fabricio Pamplona, "The Power of Visuals," MedTech Intelligence, February 8, 2023, https://medtechintelligence.com/column/the-power-of-visuals/.

† John Stevens, "How to Use the Picture Superiority Effect to Your Advantage," WordTracker, accessed September 3, 2025, https://www.wordtracker.com/academy/social/visual/how-to-use-the-picture-superiority-effect-to-your-advantage#:~:text=The%20picture%20superiority%20effect%20refers,be%20used%20in%20many%20contexts.

‡ Brett Henebery, "Using Visuals Improves Learning by Up to 400%," *The Educator*, June 23, 2022, https://www.theeducatoronline.com/k12/news/using-visuals-improves-learning-by-up-to-400—study/280453.

Applying the Exhibit Step to the Three Goals of Every Coaching Session

In the previous chapter, we started off with the first E of the 4E Coaching Method. We used the example of hearing a salesperson's pitch go up at the end of quoting the price of $1,200. You might think that explaining what you want them to do would count as coaching, but I am here to tell you it isn't enough.

The next step is for you to role-play the behavior change you want to see for them. In other words, you need to Exhibit the microskill *as though you were the salesperson.*

In the example of the salesperson's voice elevating in pitch, you would exhibit a downward pitch to him or her. To make this crystal clear, let's take E1 (Explain) from the last chapter and add E2 (Exhibit) so you can see both steps back-to-back.

E1: Explain

Sales Leader: "Let's talk about what happened when you shared the price.

"You gave the correct number, and I noticed the tone of your voice went up at the end. It came across like a question instead of a confident statement. That one vocal habit can change how the entire message is received. When we sound unsure, even slightly, the buyer starts to question whether they should be confident in us or in the price. We could have had the best presentation up to that point, but the uncertainty in our voice creates doubt.

"What we say is important, but how we say it carries just as much weight, especially when it comes to price.

"I'd like you to drop the tone at the end of the sentence, so it lands more like a fact or a confident statement rather than a question. Does that make sense to you?"

Salesperson: "Yes. I get it."

E2: Exhibit

Sales Leader: "Great. Now, let me show you the difference with me being the salesperson. In the first example, I will show you what your voice did when you gave the price, and then in the second example, I will show you the dropped tone I would like you to have instead.

"That's a good question . . . it's $1,200" (said with an upward pitch at the end).

"Did you hear the up tone when I gave the price?"

Salesperson: "Totally."

Sales Leader: "Okay. Now I want you to hear it when I drop the tone.

"That's a good question . . . the price is $1,200" (said with a dropped tonality).

"Did you hear the difference?"

Salesperson: "Wow. That's a huge difference. I didn't realize I was even doing it."

Sales Leader: "I know. That's why coaching is so important."

Using a vocal quality for E2 is a little difficult, so I am going to give you another example to make sure you really get it.

Do you remember Derek from chapter 4? You know, the guy who would reach out with his hands to ask for the sale as if he was going to choke the buyer out? Let's go back to that example to see how E1 and E2 showed up to start his performance improvement.

E1: Explain

Ryan: "Do you all mind if I give a little feedback here?"

Derek: "Sure. What's up?"

Ryan: "Well, I couldn't help but notice that as you are asking for the sale, you look like you are going to choke her out."

Derek: "Crap. I can't believe I did that."

Kat: "I've seen you do it before."

Derek: "Oh man. That's awful."

Ryan: "Well, the good news is that it's fixable. Obviously, you shouldn't have your hands out in front of you in a choking motion. Clearly that's going to cause your buyer to either feel threatened or at the least mistrust you, even if it's on a subconscious level . . . fair?"

Derek: "Totally fair."

Ryan: "I think it makes more sense for you to go totally casual when you ask for the sale. Specifically, I want you to try leaning on something like the wall or a countertop, put your hands in your pocket, and ask for the sale.

"This will show your buyer that you are confident . . . and not a weirdo. Does that make sense?"

Derek: "Yup."

E2: Exhibit

Ryan: "Awesome. Let me show you what you did, and then I will show you what I'd like you to do instead."

(I stepped in as the salesperson and mirrored back to Derek exactly what he did with the choking motion. Then I did it again, but this time I leaned back against the wall, slowly put my hands in my pockets, and said, "Well, Kat, it looks like everything lines up perfectly. Are you ready to make this home yours?")

"Okay . . . did you see the difference in the confidence?"

Derek: "I did, but I have to be honest. I was always told not to put my hands in my pockets. Was that bad advice?"

Ryan: "It seems like a pretty good option compared to choking them out."

Derek: "Fair point."

You might think that E1 and E2 are enough to create behavior change, especially when a salesperson has the revelation that they are using choking motions when asking for the sale! Well, again, it's not enough. You have to go through all four steps of the 4E Coaching Method to ensure performance improvement.

The next step is arguably where true performance improvement happens. E3: Execute!

One pro tip here is that you can use alternative ways to exhibit the proper behaviors. Let's say you have someone on your team who is really good at the microskill you are coaching. It might make sense to have the salesperson you are coaching shadow your star on that particular skill. Another way you can exhibit the right behaviors is to show your salesperson a video of the microskill being performed properly.

My advice is for you, as the sales leader, to get very comfortable stepping in to show your team how it's done rather than immediately defaulting to video and other salespeople to exhibit. This shows them that you are invested in the learning and are willing to do the work yourself. Videos and shadowing exercises are good options as well, but I challenge you to get out of your comfort zone first!

Summary

The second step of the 4E Coaching Method, Exhibit, reinforces one of the most powerful truths in learning: People don't learn just by hearing; they learn by seeing. In the same way a Rick Steves travel guide removes uncertainty for tourists, great sales coaches remove ambiguity by modeling the exact behavior they want their team to replicate. Visual learning taps into how the brain is wired, improves retention, and boosts confidence. Research shows that combining explanation with demonstration dramatically increases understanding . . . and in coaching, that's what drives transformation. When a sales leader shows what good looks like, the intangible becomes tangible and the theoretical becomes practical.

Whether you're demonstrating tone, posture, body language, or phrasing, your ability to demonstrate rather than just explain is what elevates your coaching from advice to action. As seen in real-life examples with salespeople like Derek, the Exhibit step not only clarifies expectations but creates immediate self-awareness and buy-in. And it doesn't always have to come from you. Sometimes the best exhibits come from peers, videos, or top performers. What matters is that the salesperson sees it with their own eyes. The next step is where the reps begin. It's time to Execute!

Questions to Ponder

- When was the last time you physically demonstrated a specific skill you coached . . . or did you just explain it?
- What microskills on your team are begging for a strong visual example or demonstration?
- Could you be using video, peer shadowing, or role-play more effectively to "Exhibit" in your coaching sessions?

CHAPTER TEN

THE 4E COACHING METHOD: EXECUTE

To know and not to do is not to know.

—**Ancient Chinese philosophy**

Most people would probably agree that we learn best by doing . . . and I know that's certainly true for me. But this section isn't about personal opinion or learning preferences. It's about what the science tells us without question:

Having your salesperson physically perform
the microskill you're coaching
is the single most critical part
of the development process.

Watching and listening can help, but nothing replaces execution. That's where real growth happens.

There are several compelling studies that illustrate just how essential execution is to the learning process. One of the most cited is the one I mentioned in chapter 9, and that is Edgar Dale's *Cone of Learning*. According to Dale's study, when people actively perform a task, their retention rates can climb as high as 90 percent. But the science goes even deeper than that.

In 2015, a study titled "Physical Experience Enhances Science Learning" was published by a team led by Dr. Sian Beilock, an internationally recognized expert on the mind-body connection and author of *How the Body Knows Its Mind*. The goal of the study was to explore the difference between *active* and *passive* learning . . . particularly, how learning impacts retention and brain activity.*

Participants were divided into two groups and taught the physics of angular momentum using a bicycle wheel. One group simply observed the wheel spinning while the concept was explained. The second group held the wheel in their hands and experienced the torque firsthand while hearing the same lesson.

Weeks later, both groups were tested. The students who had physically interacted with the wheel scored an average of 7 percent higher than those who had only observed. That's a meaningful difference, but the most fascinating insight came from the brain scans.

Each participant underwent a functional MRI (fMRI) during the learning process. The passive observers showed activation primarily in visual and auditory processing areas. But the active learners lit up sensorimotor regions, specifically, the motor cortex and somatosensory cortex. These are the parts of the brain responsible for movement and physical coordination.

In other words, physically doing the task recruited deeper, more engaged parts of the brain, creating a stronger neural imprint and improving long-term understanding. As Beilock put it:

* Jann Ingmire, "Learning by Doing Helps Students Perform Better in Science," UChicago News, April 29, 2015, https://news.uchicago.edu/story/learning-doing-helps-students-perform-better-science.

"Reading about a concept in a textbook or even seeing a demonstration in class is not the same as physically experiencing what you are learning about."*

The Truth

I've been coaching sales professionals for over twenty years, and I can tell you this is the hardest part of the process. Why? Because when you ask a salesperson to execute a microskill in front of you, you're asking them to perform under pressure . . . with you (their boss) watching! That naturally triggers discomfort and, often, pushback.

Think about it. Human nature drives us to defend, deflect, or avoid situations where we might feel judged. When you say, "Let's try that close again" or "Show me how you'd respond to this objection," what the salesperson might hear is "You're not doing it right." Even if your intent is developmental, the experience can feel like an attack.

So, before we dive into how to guide a salesperson through executing a microskill, we need to pause and address something critical: the soft skills of coaching. How you show up in that moment. It's crucial to understand how your tone, your posture, and your ability to create psychological safety can make or break the effectiveness of the *Execute* phase in the 4E Coaching Method.

There are three specific soft skills I leverage in just about every coaching session I do:

- Empathy
- Encouragement
- Energy

* Jann Ingmire, "Learning by Doing," 2015.

Empathy

Brené Brown defines empathy as "feeling with people."* That's the perfect mindset to bring into the Execute phase of coaching. Before you ask a salesperson to demonstrate a microskill, take a moment to put yourself in their shoes. As I mentioned earlier, even top performers can feel exposed when asked to perform something they haven't yet mastered . . . especially with their boss watching.

Empathy communicates a powerful message: "This is a safe place to mess up. We're here to develop you, not to judge you." In my seminars, I often say you can't have empathy and judgment in the same space. That being the case, it's essential to lead with empathy so the person you're coaching doesn't feel criticized or under attack.

Here's how that might sound:

"I know this part can feel a little uncomfortable, but remember, we're not aiming for perfect. We're just going to see if we can level this up a bit. Sound good?"

Using language like this softens the intensity of the moment. In essence, empathy gives them permission to try, stumble, and grow.

Encouragement

It's always amazing to me how often leaders omit encouragement from their coaching sessions. My experience is that every single person on the planet needs encouragement.

Your salesperson is no different than anyone else on the planet . . . me included! I remember when I made the decision to start my company, Impact Eighty-Eight. I had some serious doubts. I had failed in business once before, and I couldn't afford to let that happen again.

---

* Brené Brown, "Brené Brown on Empathy," posted 2014 by RSA Shorts, YouTube, https://www.youtube.com/watch?v=1Evwgu369Jw&t=2s.

I shared those concerns with my wife, Melissa. She looked at me and said something I'll never forget: "You're going to be wildly successful. Honestly, you should've done this a couple of years ago." Then she reminded me of everything I had accomplished and the impact I had already made, and finished with "If anyone can do this, it's you."

Encouragement can make all the difference in someone's success. It's about reinforcing belief in both the process and in the person. When a salesperson senses that you're in their corner, they're far more likely to step into the discomfort of execution.

Here are a few ways that might sound:

- "This is one of those small tweaks that can really shift your results. I'm excited to see how you handle it. Go ahead and give it a shot."
- "You've totally got this. If I didn't believe in you, I wouldn't be here investing this time. I know you can do it. Let's give it a try and see what happens."
- "You've got the skills. You just need a rep or two to lock it in. Let's run it once and dial it in together."

Encouragement isn't about sugarcoating; it's about instilling belief at the moment they need it most. The right words, spoken with authenticity and confidence, can unlock action and move a salesperson from average to amazing!

Energy

When I say energy is a soft skill, I'm not talking about being loud or over the top, or putting on a performance. I'm talking about the emotional presence you bring into a coaching session. You want to display the right tone, posture, and attitude that communicates "I'm here for you, and I believe in you."

Your salesperson needs to *feel* your encouragement, your excitement, and most importantly, your belief that they can do it. That level of belief isn't just something you say; it's something you transmit. Your energy should say, "You got this, and I'm in it with you 100 percent!"

You can say all the right words to encourage someone, but if you show up with flat, distracted, or even neutral energy, your salesperson will pick up on it instantly, and they'll begin to doubt whether you actually mean what you're saying. In contrast, when your energy is warm and uplifting, it makes your feedback land better, your encouragement feel real, and the overall experience more motivating.

In short, your energy creates an atmosphere where growth can happen. Make it intentional.

Pattern Interrupts

Occasionally, you'll coach a salesperson who's clearly stuck in their own head. Maybe they're hyperfocused on their workbook, glued to their script, or just overly aware that you're watching them . . . no matter how much empathy you're bringing to the moment, even if you're channeling your inner Brené Brown.

When that happens, you may need to use a technique borrowed from clinical psychology called a *pattern interrupt*. A pattern interrupt is a deliberate strategy used to disrupt someone's automatic thoughts, emotions, or behaviors. It creates a mental pause, something that snaps them out of autopilot and brings them fully into the present.

According to research published in *Clinical Psychology: Science and Practice*, clinicians use pattern interrupts to stop recurring, self-defeating cycles and redirect clients toward more adaptive thinking.* In other words, breaking the pattern creates space for better responses. In coaching, that space is where progress happens.

Examples of Pattern Interrupts

I have to admit . . . I *love* using pattern interrupts. I tend to do small group coaching sessions where I will have people partner up, and then I bounce around and coach participants one-on-one. When I find a salesperson who gets really stuck, I can't wait to use a pattern interrupt.

I recall working with a new-home salesperson in the Phoenix market named Gary. We were working on how to prescribe a specific floor plan and the price of that home. Gary, an analytical man by nature, was getting flustered in the execute stage of the 4E Coaching Method. I recall Gary saying, "This just doesn't feel right. I mean, I know what I am doing." Ultimately, Gary was too in his head, and he was actually getting worse at the technique rather than better. It was time to deploy a pattern interrupt.

I looked at Gary and said, "I get it. It's a role-play, and it isn't real life. Do me a favor and hand me your workbook real quick." Gary handed it over. I looked at it for half a second, and then I threw it across the room. I recall it startled Gary. That was exactly what I needed to have happen. I then said, "Forget the technique. Just tell me the plan that works and tell me the price. Go!"

What do you think happened?

Gary nailed it. And as you could guess, that is where the encouragement part came back into play. I told him, "Dude! That was it. You totally nailed that! Awesome job." To this day, I can recall the shift in Gary. He stood a little taller and had a sense of relief . . . not to

---

* Michael J. Rohrbaugh and Varda Shoham, "Brief Therapy Based on Interrupting Ironic Processes: The Palo Alto Model," *Clinical Psychology* 8, no. 1 (2001), https://pmc.ncbi.nlm.nih.gov/articles/PMC2789564/.

mention a smile and some swagger to match. All because I used a pattern interrupt to get him out of his head.

Here are a few examples of pattern interrupts you can use in your coaching sessions. Each is designed to snap salespeople out of mental autopilot or defensiveness and re-engage them in the moment:

1. **Ditch the Script—Literally (My #1 Technique)**

   When to use it: The salesperson is clinging to their workbook or notes like a life raft and not actually engaging with the skill.

   Interrupt: Ask, "Can I see your workbook for a second?" (Then gently toss it across the room.) "You don't need that right now. You know what to do. Trust yourself."

   Why it works: It's physical, unexpected, and symbolic. It breaks their attachment to the "rules" and forces them to be present. It sends the message: The real learning doesn't live on the page; it lives in practice.

2. **Role Reversal**

   When to use it: The salesperson is stiff, robotic, or stuck in "script mode."

   Interrupt: Say, "Okay, pause. Let's switch roles. I'll be the salesperson; you be the buyer. Let's see how it feels from your side." Essentially, you are going back one step to Exhibit as a pattern interrupt.

Why it works: It breaks the pattern of performance anxiety, creates a moment of levity, and gives them perspective . . . all while keeping the focus on skill development.

3. **Change the Environment**

   When to use it: The salesperson is visibly nervous or mentally checking out.

   Interrupt: Say, "Let's walk and talk. Grab your water. We're taking this to the showroom."

   Why it works: Physically moving to a new space resets the brain. A change in environment often leads to a change in energy and attention. This also reinforces that sales don't happen in a vacuum.

4. **Ask an Unexpected Question**

   When to use it: The salesperson is spiraling in self-doubt or stuck justifying their old behavior.

   Interrupt: Ask, "Wait . . . do you remember your best sale this month? What made that buyer say yes?"

   Why it works: This pulls their brain away from defensiveness and toward confidence. It shifts their emotional state, reconnects them to something positive, and reopens their mindset for learning.

5. **Use Humor (Light and Strategic)**

   When to use it: The salesperson is taking themselves too seriously or is visibly tense.

   Interrupt: With a smile, say, "Okay, unless this is your audition for a crime drama, let's loosen up and have some fun with it."

   Why it works: A light, playful comment breaks tension, resets their emotional state, and signals that the goal is progress, not perfection. Laughter is a powerful disruptor of performance anxiety.

6. **Call Out the Pattern (Gently)**

   When to use it: The salesperson is repeating a justification or excuse loop.

   Interrupt: "Have you noticed we've come back to that explanation a few times now? Let's pause and try something new just for sixty seconds."

   Why it works: You're not attacking the person; you're naming the pattern. This helps them become aware of their own loop and invites a short, low-risk reset.

7. **Create a "Do It Wrong" Moment (One of My Favorites!)**

   When to use it: The salesperson is paralyzed by perfectionism or fear of messing up.

Interrupt: Say, "Here's the deal . . . your only job is to do it wrong on purpose. Seriously. Let's make it the worst sales pitch ever."

Why it works: This reverses the pressure dynamic. It decreases the gravity, gets them laughing, and usually results in better performance after the playful reset.

Execute in Action

You'll remember my friend Derek from the last chapter . . . you know, the one who asked for the sale like he was acting out a murder scene with his hands outstretched as if he were about to strangle the buyer. It's hilarious in hindsight but clearly not effective.

For continuity, let's revisit how we coached Derek through E1: Explain and E2: Exhibit, and now move into the third and most critical step: E3: Execute.

E1: Explain

Ryan: "Do you all mind if I give a little feedback here?"

Derek: "Sure. What's up?"

Ryan: "Well, I couldn't help but notice that as you are asking for the sale, you look like you are going to choke her out."

Derek: "Crap. I can't believe I did that."

Kat: "I've seen you do it before."

Derek: "Oh man. That's awful."

Ryan: "Well, the good news is that it's fixable. Obviously, you shouldn't have your hands out in front of you in a choking motion. Clearly that's going to cause your buyer to feel either threatened or at the least mistrust you, even if it's on a subconscious level . . . fair?"

Derek: "Totally fair."

Ryan: "I think it makes more sense for you to go totally casual when you ask for the sale. Specifically, I want you to try leaning on something like the wall or a countertop, put your hands in your pocket, and ask for the sale.

"This will show your buyer that you are confident . . . and not a weirdo. Does that make sense?"

Derek: "Yup."

E2: Exhibit

Ryan: "Awesome. Let me show you what you did, and then I will show you what I'd like you to do instead.

(I stepped in as the salesperson and mirrored back to Derek exactly what he did with the choking motion. Then I did it again, but this time I leaned back against the wall, slowly put my hands in my pockets, and said, "'Well, Kat, it looks like everything lines up perfectly. Are you ready to make this home yours?")

"Okay . . . did you see the difference in the confidence?"

Derek: "I did, but I have to be honest, I was always told not to put my hands in my pockets. Was that bad advice?"

Ryan: "It seems like a pretty good option compared to choking them out."

Derek: "Fair point."

E3: Execute

Ryan: "Okay . . . This will likely feel awkward to you, and that's okay. Let's just give it a shot and see what happens. That being said, let's have you step back into the salesperson role, and this time, you're going to lean back slowly, put your hands in your pockets, and ask if she wants to buy the home."

Derek: "Okay. I'll give it a try."

Ryan: "I am confident you're going to feel the difference. You got this!"

Derek stepped into the role, paused for a moment, and said, "Okay, with that in mind, are you ready to take the home off the market?" He instinctively started to lean forward but then caught himself and leaned back against the wall as he finished the line.

Honestly, it was pretty good. But the moment he finished, Derek shook his head and said, "Ohh, that was terrible. It just feels so awkward." Then he grabbed his workbook and buried his eyes in it like it held the answer to all life's problems.

We went back and forth for a bit, and I could tell he was stuck in his own head. That was when I knew a pattern interrupt was needed. So I decided to go with one of my favorites: Ditch the Script.

I said, "Can I see your workbook real quick?" Derek handed it over. I glanced at it . . . and then launched it out of the room.

I looked at him and said, "Forget the sale. Just ask while leaning back." Then I gave him my three favorite words in coaching:

"Do it again."

(You'll hear more about that in chapter 12.)

Summary

Execution is where coaching creates transformation. While explaining and exhibiting are essential, they don't create lasting change on their own. True performance improvement happens when the salesperson physically performs the skill. In other words, when they *do the thing*. This phase of the 4E Coaching Method can be uncomfortable for both the coach and salesperson, but it's where all the prep work pays off. It's also where your soft skills—empathy, encouragement, and energy—play a critical role in creating a safe space for practice and progress.

As a coach, your job isn't to make execution easy; it's to make it possible. That means creating the right emotional environment, offering consistent belief, and when needed, breaking unproductive patterns that hold people back. Coaching someone through execution takes patience, but it also takes boldness. Don't be afraid to challenge. Don't be afraid to interrupt. And never underestimate how powerful it is to say "Do it again."

Questions to Ponder

- When was the last time you coached a salesperson all the way through execution, not just explanation or observation?
- What emotional cues (defensiveness, nervousness, checking out) do you tend to overlook that might signal a need for a pattern interrupt?
- How can you better use your tone, posture, or physical presence to project belief and safety during the Execute phase?

CHAPTER ELEVEN

THE 4E COACHING METHOD: EVALUATE

Feedback is the breakfast of champions.

—Ken Blanchard

Let's assume you're back on the sales floor. You walk into your sales office after a long weekend. You're still thinking about the couple who *nearly* bought on Saturday . . . and the fact that they didn't. Before you can settle in, your sales leader pulls you aside and says with a very direct and urgent tone:

> "Hey, we need to talk. I watched your presentation on Saturday, and honestly . . . it just wasn't good. You were kind of all over the place. You've got to tighten things up, or we're going to lose buyers."

That's it. No examples. No specifics. No direction.

What's your gut reaction?

Do you feel motivated to improve?

Do you have clarity on what to do next?

Are you remotely inspired to try something different?

Or do you feel defensive? Confused? Maybe even a little defeated?

Poor feedback isn't just unhelpful; it's destructive. It leaves people guessing, second-guessing, and stuck in the dark. And sadly, it happens all the time in sales leadership. Not because managers don't care, but because they haven't been trained on how to evaluate performance in a way that leads to growth.

The final step in the 4E Coaching Method, *Evaluate*, is about shining a light on what happened, what improved, and what needs attention next. **It's not about judgment**. It's about clarity. It's how we close the loop on the coaching process and help our people build true confidence . . . not from hype, but from evidence.

The WIN Feedback Framework

Too many sales leaders start giving feedback with what needs to change right out of the gate. The reason is we love to solve problems. The challenge is it comes across as being critical. The key to making sure you don't deflate your sales team is to use what I call the WIN framework.

W—What Went Well?

As you watch your salesperson Execute the microskill you coached during E1 and E2, there's a good chance they implemented some, or even all, of your direction. The key here is to recognize that improvement. Be specific, sincere, and behavior focused. It might sound like this:

> "Jordan, great job using the closing framework. You added the bridge phrase perfectly, and I really liked how you dropped your tone when you asked for the sale. That's a massive improvement from where you started!"

The *W* in WIN matters because we all crave recognition. In my seminars, I often reference the old saying that "babies cry for it, and grown men die for it." Your salespeople are no different.

When you get the behaviors right, the sales plan builds itself.

But here's the mistake we often make in sales: We recognize the wrong thing . . . *the results*. You've been in those meetings. You know the ones:

"Let's give it up for Bill. He made ten sales this week!"

Cue the polite golf clap while half the room silently curses Bill for having the best store with the highest traffic.

I'm not against recognizing results, but I'm a bigger fan of recognizing the behaviors that drive them. When you get the behaviors right, the sales plan builds itself.

Recognizing What Went Well isn't just a feel-good leadership ploy, it's a performance lever. When a salesperson nails part of the microskill you've been coaching, your job is to catch it and reinforce it.

Why? Because recognition builds confidence and it builds results.

A field study conducted by researchers at Duke University and the University of Texas found that public recognition (without any financial incentive) led to a *measurable increase in performance*. The employees who were recognized saw a significant productivity boost, and that improvement spread to their peers. In other words: Recognition is contagious, and it pays off.*

So, when you see the behavior you've been coaching show up, even if it's just a partial improvement, don't wait. Say something and reinforce the win.

Catch the behavior. Celebrate the effort. Reinforce the growth.

---

* Jana Gallus and Bruno S. Frey, "Awards: A Strategic Management Perspective," *Strategic Management Journal* 37, no. 8 (August 2016): 1699–1714.

Remember that what gets recognized gets repeated, and what gets repeated gets results.

Later in this chapter, we will get into the soft skills of coaching via your tone and how to be more on the inspirational side without being a motivational speaker.

I—Insight

Just because your salesperson made it through the 4Es and heard your feedback doesn't mean the lesson has fully landed. Growth doesn't happen from hearing alone . . . It happens through thinking and processing.

That's why the next step is for you to ask for your salesperson's *Insight.*

Getting Insight isn't about reteaching. In fact, it's not about you talking at all. It's about creating an opportunity for reflection. The goal is to help salespeople connect the dots between the new actions they tried in the Execute step and the new potential outcomes. Insight locks in the learning and builds ownership.

Here's how you do that. Right after you point out the W, what went right, you then ask for the salesperson to share his or her thoughts. For example, you might ask:

- "What felt different when you tried it that way?"
- "Looking back, what part felt strongest to you?"
- "If you had that conversation again, what might you do differently?"

When they reflect out loud, the learning has a much greater chance of sticking. And more importantly, your sales team, not just you, takes responsibility for it.

N—Next Time

After you've reinforced What Went Well and helped your salesperson gain Insight, it's time to move to the final piece of the WIN framework: Next Time.

This is where you shift the conversation from reflection to application. Think of it as setting the GPS for the next performance moment. You're answering the question, "What's the next small improvement you'll make the next time you're in this situation?"

This step matters because learning without action is wasted effort. If your salesperson leaves the conversation thinking, "That was nice coaching" but doesn't have a Next Time action in mind, the coaching session didn't create growth; it just created a pleasant chat.

Next Time is about locking in a commitment to the next microskill tweak, the next behavior to practice, or the next layer of improvement.

Here's what that might sound like:

- "Next time you're with a customer, how will you make that bridge phrase sound even more natural?"
- "What's one small adjustment you'll make next time to help the buyer visualize their life in the home?"
- "Next time you present price, how will you slow your pace even further to create more gravity?"

Notice the pattern. These aren't demands. They're cocreated action steps. You're inviting the salesperson to decide with you what happens next.

And here's the key: Keep it small. Microskills are called micro for a reason. Don't try to fix everything at once. One improvement at a time is how mastery is built.

The WIN Framework Recap

W—What Went Well?
I—Insight: What did you learn?
N—Next Time: What's the next small improvement?

When you use WIN consistently, you create a coaching culture that's positive, where people want to learn and grow. You move away from "boss telling salesperson what they did wrong" and toward a culture of growth and learning.

Feedback shouldn't feel like a performance review or a nag session; it should feel like a conversation that encourages and lifts up your salespeople.

Critical Coaching Versus Collaborative Coaching

Having a great framework is one thing; delivering it in a way that doesn't feel like you're nitpicking or beating up your team is another skill entirely.

In my experience, most sales leaders have the best intentions. But in the rush to drive results, it's easy to slip into critical coaching. Think critical parenting or being a critical spouse. No one responds well to that . . . not at home, and certainly not on your sales team.

That's why one of the goals of every coaching session is to help your team improve how *they* communicate. Earlier, we talked about three key areas to watch:

- Words
- Vocal qualities
- Body language

But here's the thing: The same rules apply to you as a coach.

The best frameworks won't save you if your tone feels condescending, if your body language is closed off, or if your words sound more like criticism than collaboration. Coaching isn't just about what you say; it's about how you make your salesperson feel when you say it.

The alternative is *collaborative coaching*. That's when you create a space where the salesperson feels safe to reflect, own their growth, and stay engaged in the process. Collaborative coaching doesn't mean soft coaching—it means coaching with, not at.

Let me break this down with some real examples.

The chart on Page 116 is a side-by-side look at how a coach might deliver feedback on the same microskill, but in two very different ways. One leads to defensiveness. The other builds confidence and inspires action.

The Evaluate step is where coaching either creates breakthroughs or breakdowns.

Critical coaching feels like correction, and I guarantee it will lead to your sales team shutting down. In contrast, collaborative coaching feels like you are partnering with your team, and it will lead to performance improvement.

Remember: Your tone, body language, and words signal whether you're trying to catch someone failing or coach someone forward.

You could say all the right things, but if your tone is sharp, you let out a sigh of frustration, or you rub your face when a salesperson just "isn't getting it," you're being critical in a nonverbal way. And that's just as damaging as using the wrong words.

The goal is alignment. Your words, vocal qualities, and body language should all communicate the same message:

I believe in you. You've got this. And I'm here to help.

When you coach from that place, your team won't run from coaching—they'll run toward improvement.

Microskill Being Coached	Critical Coaching (Creates Defensiveness)	Collaborative Coaching (Builds Confidence and Action)
Pacing the Close	"You rushed the close again. We've talked about this. Why aren't you slowing down?"	"I noticed you picked up your pace at the end. Let's work on slowing your tone to create more gravity in the close. How did that feel to you?"
Asking Discovery Questions	"You didn't ask enough questions. That's why you're not connecting with the buyer."	"You had a few solid discovery questions today. Let's build on that . . . What's one or two more you could add next time to get deeper into their 'why'?"
Handling Objections with Curiosity	"You jumped straight to defending the price. That's not the way to handle objections."	"I could see you wanted to resolve the price objection quickly. Next time, let's try staying curious a little longer. What's one question you could ask first to understand their concern better?"
Using Visual Demonstration	"That walk was just you talking. It wasn't a real demonstration, and we need to do better."	"You did a nice job describing features. Let's make it even more interactive next time. What's one way you could bring it to life for the buyer?"
Transitioning to Next Steps	"You left the next step too open, and that's how deals fall apart."	"I loved how you wrapped up the visit. Let's tighten the close by locking in the next step before the buyer leaves. What might that sound like in your own words?"

Summary

The Evaluate step is where coaching comes full circle. It's not just about pointing out mistakes or celebrating wins; it's about guiding your salesperson through reflection and setting a clear path for what happens next. The WIN framework gives you a simple, powerful way to do that by focusing on what went well, gaining insight, and cocreating the next step. When you coach this way, you build better performance, and you build trust, ownership, and long-term growth.

But frameworks alone aren't enough. Delivery matters just as much as content. If your tone, body language, and words feel critical or harsh, your salesperson will shut down. If they feel collaborative, supported, and safe, they'll lean in and grow. Coaching isn't about catching someone doing something wrong. It's about catching them in the act of getting better, reinforcing it, and helping them take the next step forward.

Questions to Ponder

- When you give feedback, do you tend to lead with correction or with recognition?
- How often do you create space for your sales team to reflect and share their own insights before you give direction?
- Are your body language, tone, and word choice consistently signaling, "I believe in you, and I'm here to help"? If not, what are you signaling?

CHAPTER TWELVE

"DO IT AGAIN!" YOUR THREE NEW FAVORITE WORDS

I fear not the man who has practiced 10,000 kicks once, but I fear the man who has practiced one kick 10,000 times.

—Bruce Lee

Imagine there is a sales leader named Debbie who is working through the 4E Coaching Method with a fairly seasoned sales rep named Johann. During the coaching process, Johann gets visibly frustrated with the fact that he has to "role-play." In his words, he says, "Why are you making me do this? I know how to sell."

What might Debbie be tempted to do at the end of the 4E framework? If you thought *End the coaching session*, you'd likely be right. And that would be the completely wrong thing to do! You see, coaching isn't about one rep of practice or checking the box; it's about repetition and improvement along the way.

For me as a coach of more than two decades, this is arguably the most pivotal moment in performance improvement coaching. If you stop right here, the learning won't stick. I can just about guarantee it.

So what should happen after you end the 4E coaching process? Simply put, have your salesperson *do it again*!

The Power of Repetition

I believe we all understand the power of repetition at some level. Whether you were forced to play an instrument as a kid or you were passionate about a sport, you knew one truth: If you wanted to get better, you had to practice.

Oddly enough, a large number of sales professionals don't see practice the same way. They'll say things like "I like to be organic when talking to a customer" or "I've been selling for years. I know what I'm doing."

I get it—practice can feel uncomfortable, especially when you've been doing the job for a long time. But as we highlighted in chapter 5, experience doesn't always equal growth. Remember Nick? He had thirty years on the job, but in reality, he had one year repeated thirty times. He was the guy who refused to practice or develop new skills.

So what does repetition actually do for your team?

Sure, your salespeople will gain new skills, but it goes further than that. There's real science behind it. Repetition builds stronger neural connections. Each time a skill is repeated, whether it's practicing a confidence close or overcoming a specific objection, the brain gets a clear message:

"Pay attention. This matters."

When that happens, the brain starts to reinforce those circuits. It actually builds stronger "wiring" for whatever microskill is being practiced. There's even a physical change happening: An insulating layer called myelin wraps around neural pathways, making them faster and more efficient. That's the foundation of what scientists call *automaticity* . . . when actions stop feeling forced and start feeling natural.

Repetition also shifts learning from the prefrontal cortex (where thinking is slow and effortful) to the basal ganglia (the habit and action center). That's when mastery shows up, and the only way to move a skill from one part of the brain to the other is through practice.

Think of it like driving a car from the prefrontal cortex to the basal ganglia. The fuel that makes the trip possible? Repetition.

The Ed Sheeran Story—Mastery Through Reps

Before Ed Sheeran filled stadiums, he filled coffee shops, pubs, street corners, and living rooms. While most new musicians were hustling for a single weekly gig, Sheeran took a different path: He played three shows a day.

Every single day.

In his early days, Sheeran wasn't the polished performer we know today. He's admitted in interviews that his first recordings were rough . . . sometimes embarrassingly so. But instead of letting that stop him, he used those early, awkward performances as fuel. He kept the recordings as proof of how far practice and repetition could take him.

If you want to take a listen (I mean literally hear a recording of how terrible he was), check out his interview on the Jonathan Ross Show. You can find it on YouTube under the title "Ed Sheeran Singing Badly."

Sheeran once told NPR: "When people say artists are born with talent, you're not. You have to really learn and really practice. My first recordings were terrible, but I kept at it. I did about a thousand shows before anyone cared."

He often slept on couches or even subway station floors just to keep the cycle going. Why? Because repetition builds more than skill. It builds stamina, presence, timing, confidence, and authenticity.

It's not just about playing the song . . . It's about learning how to deliver it when you're tired, when the room is empty, when the mic cuts out, or when someone interrupts you. Sheeran learned to thrive in all conditions because he did it again and again and again.

That's how mastery happens.

That's how your authentic voice emerges.

The Power of Accountability

In the fall of 2023, I was leading a two-day new-home-sales training seminar in Phoenix. At the end of the session, a salesperson named Charlie approached me and said, "Can I ask for your help?"

That's a great question, not because it flatters me, but because so few people are willing to ask for help in the first place. Most of us pretend we have it all figured out. We don't want to admit when we're stuck, and we're afraid of looking stupid.

Not Charlie.

Charlie has this rugged look, beard and all, but still comes across as one of the nicest guys you'll ever meet. Picture a teddy bear who probably knows how to camp, fix his own truck, and change the oil on an old Camaro.

I asked Charlie what he needed help with specifically. During the training, I'd focused on two main topics:

1. Getting the buyer's story
2. Asking for the sale on the first visit (which, let's be honest, is a common problem in sales)

Charlie said, "Well . . . I think I'm pretty good at getting the story. Where I'm struggling is asking for the sale."

At that point, Charlie had gone a few weeks without a sale and was getting nervous. If I remember correctly, he'd just had "the talk" with his sales manager.

I asked him point-blank, "Do you really want to fix this?"

He said yes.

So I hit him with a pretty hard truth: "Charlie, the problem is that you're a customer service guy sitting in a salesperson's chair."

He paused for a second, then said, "I hate to admit it, but you're right."

Charlie asked me how we fix it, and that was when we made a plan.

I said, "I want you to text me every day you're on the sales floor. I only want you to tell me two things: (1) how many people came in (your traffic), and (2) how many of them you asked to buy."

That's it. Simple. Measurable. Repeatable.

Charlie agreed, and on November 30, we started.

Here is a screenshot of the first text:

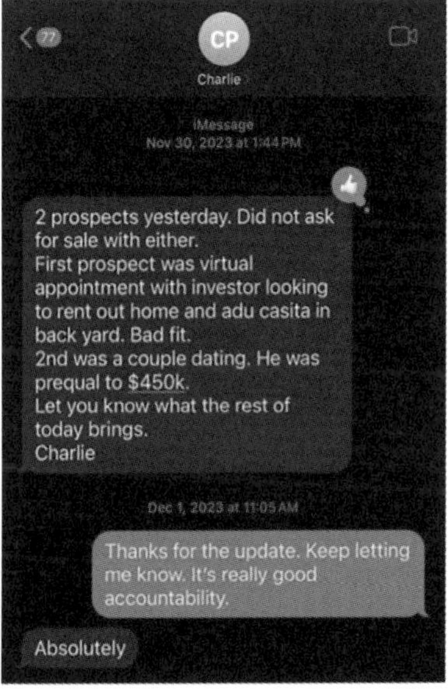

The first few texts were full of "I didn't ask."

This went on for about a week. And then . . . Charlie asked for the sale! He didn't get it, but that wasn't the point. I celebrated the behavior, not the result.

Charlie kept texting me every single day he was on the floor throughout the year. And then, at the Arizona HBACA MAME Awards (which is the Oscars for home building), they announced the Salesperson of the Year.

The winner? Charlie.

Charlie moved to another company in early 2025, became the top producer within thirty days, and continues to crush his competition.

If you're wondering how powerful accountability is, here's what Charlie had to say:

> Ryan Taft changed the trajectory of my career. I was a good new-home salesperson but hit a slump. When I reached out to Ryan, he coached me with consistent tweaks and **held me accountable with daily check-ins**. I'm proud to say I won HBACA MAME Salesperson of the Year last year . . .

This isn't about me. It's about the power of accountability and repetition coming together to drive massive performance improvement.

And the last check-in text I got from Charlie?

That came in today—July 17th, 2025.

4E x 10

When you finish the 4E Coaching Method—Explain, Exhibit, Execute, Evaluate—you might think, "Well, that's done."

But here's the reality: One round of coaching doesn't fix anything.

Maybe your salesperson improved one of the three core coaching goals.

Maybe they finally got the framework down.

Maybe they started to find their authentic voice or made progress on their communication.

But let's be real . . . odds are extremely high that they didn't improve everything.

And the odds are even higher that they haven't mastered the microskill you're working on.

So what happens next?

You do it again.

What exactly do you repeat? The entire 4E cycle.

1. **Explain:** Tell them what else you observed and where there's still room for improvement.
2. **Exhibit:** Model the behavior again so they have a clear, visual example to follow.
3. **Execute:** Let them do it again. Reps, reps, reps.
4. **Evaluate:** Use the WIN feedback framework to break it down and guide the next step.

And then what do you do?

Do it again.

Then again.

And again.

And again.

This is how mastery is built. Again, not through a single coaching session, but through 4E on repeat. Think of it as 4E x 10 (or maybe x 100). That's the real path to behavior change and performance improvement.

Summary

Mastery doesn't happen in a single moment; it happens in the repetition. That's why the best sales leaders and coaches don't just run the

4E Coaching Method once; they run it over and over again. Each round builds stronger neural connections, sharper instincts, and deeper confidence. Repetition isn't busy work; it's how the brain learns, how habits stick, and how authentic voice develops. From Ed Sheeran playing three shows a day to Charlie transforming his career through daily accountability, the formula is the same: Do it again.

The combination of repetition and accountability is what separates good from great. It's not about perfection in a single session . . . It's about committing to the process until the skill becomes second nature. Coaching isn't a one-time event; it's a continuous cycle of Explain, Exhibit, Execute, and Evaluate. And when you're done? You run the cycle again. Your new three favorite words should be *do it again*!

Questions to Ponder

- What's a skill you've taught your team that still needs another round (or ten) of 4E coaching?
- How can you build daily or weekly accountability into your coaching process, the way Charlie did?
- Are you willing to embrace the discomfort of repetition in your own leadership, just like you expect your team to?

CHAPTER THIRTEEN

TRUST, BUT VERIFY . . . ACTUALLY, JUST VERIFY

What gets inspected gets respected.

—Old business proverb

Let's assume you've just wrapped up a coaching session with one of your average-performing salespeople. You went through the 4E Coaching Method . . . maybe even ran it multiple times, and for the moment, their performance has leveled up significantly.

Then you leave.

But you don't leave empty handed. You leave with a handful of assumptions:

- They've got it 100 percent.
- They'll remember everything.
- Habits are built in one coaching session.

Guess what? You couldn't be more wrong.

The truth is that people forget, they get comfortable, and other priorities push growth to the back burner. That includes your sales team, even if you just delivered the best freaking coaching session of your life!

I know what you're thinking.

"Ryan, what the heck? I've been reading this book, implementing the chapters, doing the work, and now you're telling me it won't stick? That's lame."

Hold on, turbo. I'm not saying all is lost. I'm saying there's more work to do. Here's why.

After every coaching session, three forces immediately start working against you:

1. The Trap of Assumed Progress
2. The Hawthorne Effect
3. The Law of Least Effort

If you don't account for these, your coaching won't stick. But if you understand them and build your leadership process around them, you'll create real, lasting change.

The Trap of Assumed Progress

This antigrowth force is pretty straightforward, but it's a trap most sales leaders fall into at some point. You coach a salesperson, and during the session, they show real improvement. Perhaps they level up leaps and bounds better than before the coaching session. You leave the meeting feeling good and thinking, "Cool. They've got it now."

I am here to tell you that improvement in the moment does not necessarily equal long-term change. It's easy to get hopeful when you see someone nail a new skill during a coaching session, but one good rep doesn't create a habit. Mastery only happens through massive repetition. And by massive, I mean multiple coaching sessions, lots of practice, and real-world application.

Instead of thinking of it as permanent progress, think of it as temporary progress. They've got it today, but odds are high they'll slip back into old habits tomorrow unless there's a follow-up plan in place. Your job isn't just to coach once; it's to create a system of reinforcement so the skill actually sticks.

The Hawthorne Effect

In 1924, a team of researchers from Harvard led by Elton Mayo began a series of studies at the Western Electric Hawthorne Works in Cicero, Illinois. The original goal was to measure how different workplace conditions, like lighting, rest breaks, and hours affected employee productivity.

What they discovered was surprising. It wasn't the physical changes in the work environment that made the biggest difference. The real driver of improved performance was the attention employees received from management and researchers during the study. In other words, workers felt noticed and valued, so they tried harder.

The phenomenon became known as the Hawthorne Effect: When people know they're being observed, they tend to improve their behavior or effort temporarily. But once the observation ends and when the attention fades, performance often slips back to its original levels.*

In a nutshell, if you don't follow up to measure the success of your coaching and focus on creating a habit, odds are very high the coaching won't stick!

---

* Ayesh Perera, "Hawthorne Effect: Definition, How It Works, and How to Avoid It," Simply Psychology, February 13, 2024, https://www.simplypsychology.org/hawthorne-effect.html.

The Law of Least Effort

In my trainings, I often tell salespeople, "Your biggest competitor isn't another company; it's yourself." Specifically, it's your human nature. That's where the Law of Least Effort comes in.

Originally called the Principle of Least Effort, this idea was introduced by Harvard linguist George Zipf in 1949. His research showed that humans are hardwired to conserve energy. As a linguist, Zipf saw this in the way we naturally shorten words. Instead of saying "going to," we say "gonna." We do it without thinking. And it's everywhere today, especially when we text. Just look at how we communicate:

- BRB
- LOL
- IYKYK
- TBH
- SMH

Why do we do this? Because it's easier. And the brain loves easy.

Over the years, this concept has expanded beyond linguistics. Behavioral economist Daniel Kahneman built on it in his book *Thinking, Fast and Slow*. Kahneman describes how the brain defaults to System 1 thinking—fast, intuitive, automatic. It actively avoids System 2 thinking, which is slower, more analytical, and requires real effort.* Learning a new sales skill? That's System 2. Reverting back to your old presentation style because it feels comfortable? That's System 1.

I see the Law of Least Effort at play all the time. Let's say someone has a goal to lose weight before a wedding. They hit the gym, cut carbs, stop drinking, and do whatever it takes to get into shape. Then the wedding happens, the photos are snapped, and right after that, the

* Daniel Kahneman, *Thinking, Fast and Slow* (Farrar, Straus and Giroux, 2011).

cake shows up. This is where the Law of Least Effort kicks in. IYKYK! We try to maintain the result, but we shortcut the effort it took to get there. And as you likely know, that never works.

> What you focus on gets magnified.

As a sales manager, it's critical to recognize that your team will face this same temptation after coaching. They'll learn the new skill, show improvement in front of you, and then default back to old habits because it's easier. That's why you can't just coach—you have to follow up and verify. Without reinforcement, the Law of Least Effort will win, and the progress you worked so hard to build will fade away.

The question is: How do you keep the momentum going and develop actual performance habits?

The Power of Postcoaching Assignments

In my seminars, I often say, "What you focus on gets magnified." And if that's true—and I believe it is—then it's your job as a sales leader to help your team stay focused on mastering the new skills they learned during the 4E coaching session. Not just during the session, but after the session, when real habit building begins.

After you complete a 4E coaching session, the next step is to assign your salesperson some light homework. Not because they have extra time on their hands, but because practice between sessions dramatically increases retention and accelerates skill development. As I said, without it, the new behavior is likely to fade.

A simple way to frame this with your team is to say something along the lines of this:

"Let's make sure this sticks. Between now and our next session, I want you to work on [insert assignment]. We'll review it together and keep building from there. Sound good?"

Here are some examples of coaching assignments you can give:

- Watch a specific YouTube video on a related skill and send you a summary of the key takeaways.
- Record themselves practicing the new skill (using their phone or computer) and submit it for review.
- Shadow a top-performing salesperson and report back with three things they observed and how they'll apply them.
- Read a chapter from a book or blog post you recommend and explain how it connects to the coaching.
- Write out a role-play script or talk track and rehearse it multiple times into a voice recorder.
- Set up a peer practice session with another team member and share feedback notes afterward.

These assignments aren't busywork—they're tools to help your salesperson solidify the skills, build confidence, and make the new behavior stick.

Schedule a Follow-Up!

One of the biggest mistakes managers make in coaching (assuming the coaching happens at all) is failing to schedule a follow-up. I get it. You're busy. But you should never be too busy to follow up on the coaching you've delivered.

Let's say you conduct a 4E session with one of your team members. You wrap it up feeling good, but you leave without locking in a follow-up time. The next week, you bump into that salesperson at a sales rally, or maybe they swing by corporate and catch you at your desk. The conversation sounds like this:

Sales Manager: "Hey, Tony, how's it going?"

Tony: "Pretty good. Traffic's picked up a bit, so no complaints."

Sales Manager: "Well, that's good to hear. Let me know if you need anything."

And that's it. No check-in on the coaching. No review of the new skill. No mention of the practice.

Now, what do you think Tony is thinking? Odds are high he's wondering if the coaching was just another meeting that didn't matter. To him, it feels like you've already moved on. And without knowing it, you've just triggered both the Law of Least Effort and the Hawthorne Effect:

- Tony will naturally drift back to old habits because it's easier.
- He'll assume the skill isn't that important since no one's checking in.

If I can be honest rather than nice here, you are the problem. You are stopping the learning.

What to Do Instead

At the end of your 4E coaching session, take the same advice I give salespeople when they're with a prospect: BAMFAM.

That stands for Book a Meeting from a Meeting.

My hairstylist, Rachel at Phantom Phades in Gilbert, Arizona, is a pro at this. She won't let me leave without booking my next haircut.

In fact, she's so good at BAMFAM that I currently have twelve appointments already on the books. That's the next twelve haircuts locked in.

You need to do the same thing with your sales team. As you assign the light homework, say something like this:

> "Let's get back together to review this and run it again. I'm open Tuesday morning or Wednesday afternoon—which works better for you?"

But here's the key: Pick an exact time. If you don't nail down a specific day and time, it's not really an appointment—it's a maybe. And maybes don't get results.

Then decide on the format.

- Will it be a Zoom call?
- In-person?
- A recorded video review?
- Maybe a quick phone call?

When your team knows you're circling back to check progress, a few things happen:

- They stay focused on the new skill.
- The Hawthorne Effect doesn't get a chance to fade their performance.
- And the odds of real, lasting improvement skyrocket.

This isn't micromanagement . . . It's leadership with follow-through. It tells your team: "I'm serious about your growth, and I'm here to help make it happen."

The Certainty Test

Imagine for a moment that sales are down. Depending on when you're reading this, that might be happening right now. Suddenly, a meeting request pops up on your calendar from your CEO, company owner, or division president. The subject line says only two words:

Let's Talk.

You and I both know this isn't going to be a friendly catch-up. In fact, this could be *the* meeting—you know, the one that determines whether you keep your job!

If you're a sales leader, it's not a matter of ***if*** this moment will happen in your career—it's a matter of ***when***. The real question is how do you prepare for it?

Let's first agree on one thing: You can't walk into that meeting without answers. Fair?

So, what answers should you have?

Most sales leaders default to talking about traffic. Maybe they'll say, "We need better signage," or, "The team is really giving it their all." But let's be honest—that's not what your CEO or owner is listening for. They're sitting across from you thinking, "I wonder if this sales leader can actually get us there."

That means you need to show up with more than a market report and a thinly veiled handoff to marketing. You need to look them in the eye and say, with absolute confidence:

"My team is, without a doubt, taking every lead as far as it will go."

And here's the moment you've been preparing for, because they're going to fire back with the one question that matters most:

"How do you know?"

At that point, you'll have two options.

You can say, "That's what I believe," or you can say this:

> "I know because I've seen it. I've personally watched every member of my team perform the skills we've coached. Each of them can explain why now is the right time to buy. Each of them can handle their top three objections using our objection framework. They've all demonstrated it in practice, and I've seen it live. Their CRM notes are detailed, they are asking for the sale with confidence, their follow-up is personalized, and I've verified every step myself."

That's leadership certainty. And that's how you keep your seat at the table.

Different Ways to Verify Performance Improvement

You might be wondering, How am I supposed to find the time to verify that my entire team knows all the things (as the kids say)? #dokidsstillsaythat

The good news is, you've already done part of this work. Back in chapter 4, we talked about the different ways to uncover what needs to be coached. Well, you can use those same methods to verify that the coaching is sticking.

Here's a list of ways to verify performance improvement:

- Sit in on a live sales presentation or model tour and observe the new skill in action.
- Listen to recorded phone calls or virtual appointments.
- Watch role-play sessions where the rep demonstrates the skill back to you.

- Have team members submit a video or voice recording of themselves practicing the new behavior.
- Use mystery shops to test real-life performance.
- Get peer feedback from shadow sessions or practice pods.
- Review CRM notes to confirm personalized follow-up is happening.
- Conduct a quick stand-up meeting and ask the team to demo the new technique.
- Follow up with buyers and ask for feedback on their experience.

Verification doesn't have to be complicated or time consuming. It just has to be intentional. Start building these checkpoints into your routine in order to shift from *trusting* that progress has happened to *verifying* that it actually has.

Summary

Coaching without follow-up is like planting a seed and never watering it . . . You might see a little growth at first, but it won't last. Unfortunately, most managers fall into the trap of assumed progress. They see improvement in the moment and think the job is done. But lasting behavior change doesn't happen in one session; it happens through repetition, reinforcement, and accountability. That's why postcoaching assignments and scheduled follow-ups aren't optional; they're essential.

Your job as a sales leader is to create certainty, not guesswork. When your CEO asks, "How do you know your team is doing everything they can to close sales?" you need to have a confident answer.

And that answer comes from verification. It doesn't come from guessing or hoping that they are doing the job.

Questions to Ponder

- Are you coaching for short-term improvement or long-term habit change?
- What systems do you currently have in place to verify that your team is applying what you've coached?
- How would you answer your CEO if they asked you today, "How do you know your team is taking every sale as far as it will go?"

CHAPTER FOURTEEN

THE CALENDAR DISEASE

You will never change your life
until you change something you do daily.
The secret of your success
is found in your daily routine.

—John C. Maxwell

Recently, I was in Austin, Texas, working with a sales team on how to overcome objections. During one of the group activities, the sales manager—let's call her Tonya—pulled me aside.

Tonya started venting about her team. She said things like

"I just don't get why these guys can't do what I'm telling them to do."

"We keep stumbling over the same issues. I feel like I'm in Groundhog Day!"

"A few of them get it, but the majority are a little on the slow side."

When she finished, I asked Tonya a simple question: "Can I see your calendar?"

That caught her off guard.

Maybe other trainers had nodded sympathetically or even joined in on the complaining. But by asking to see her calendar, I was signaling something different: I wasn't going to focus on her team's effort. I was going to focus on hers.

Tonya opened her laptop and pulled up her calendar. And the problem jumped off the screen.

Any guess what it was?

There wasn't a single preplanned coaching session on her calendar. What was on there? A wall-to-wall schedule of meetings:

- Purchasing meeting
- Marketing meeting
- New communities planning session
- Sales rally prep
- Starts-and-closings update

You get the idea.

I asked her a direct question:

> "How can you complain about your team's performance if you're not helping them improve?"

Tonya gave me a surprised look, almost like she couldn't believe I wasn't going to just commiserate with her.

Then I said:

"Your job is to generate more revenue for the company. And the way you do that is through performance improvement. That isn't going to happen by itself."

She got it. But her next question is the one I hear from sales leaders all the time:

"How am I supposed to find time to do all this coaching?"

That's what the rest of this chapter is about.

Why Coaching Doesn't Happen

Most sales leaders have the right intentions. They genuinely want to help their team succeed. The issue isn't usually about desire . . . It's about habits and standards.

When I meet sales leaders who aren't actively coaching for performance improvement, it typically comes down to three common problems (assuming they know how to coach in the first place):

- A lack of intentionality
- Competing meetings and events
- Incorrect prioritization

A Lack of Intentionality

I want you to stop for a second and look at your calendar. Seriously, put the book down, grab your phone or open your laptop, and pull up next week.

Take inventory of what's scheduled . . . and what isn't.

If your calendar isn't filled with coaching sessions, and you're a front-line sales leader, then you've got some work to do.

I honestly don't know how anyone operates without a calendar. Mine is open on my computer at all times. In fact, my wife jokes that I'll send her a calendar invite just to plan a date night. But here's why:

If it's important, it gets scheduled. That's intentionality.

Coaching is not something you do when you "find time." It's something you make time for, on purpose, in advance.

There are two key activities you need to schedule with intention:

- **Pipeline Impact Calls** (covered back in chapter 4): These are one-hour blocks throughout the week where you collaborate on how to get customers over the finish line, gather intel, and uncover coaching opportunities.
- **Coaching Sessions:** These are the moments when you actually help your salespeople get better.

Remember, there are three types of coaching sessions you should be scheduling regularly:

- One-on-one coaching
- Small group coaching
- Large group coaching

If you don't intentionally block time for these, they won't happen. And if they don't happen, neither will performance improvement.

Competing Meetings and Events

In the summer of 2004, I walked into my office and opened my calendar to a completely blank day. Not one single meeting was scheduled. I felt like an artist staring at a brand-new canvas.

Looking back, I had delusions of grandeur. I was going to knock out my entire to-do list, develop a killer sales rally agenda, and who knows, maybe even get to inbox zero. #pipedream

But then the meeting invites started rolling in. First, a "quick catch-up" with marketing. Then, a debrief with my VP of sales. And then came the one that really pushed me over the edge: The purchasing department wanted me to join the review committee for new bathtubs and shower stalls. #punchmeintheface

Now, here's the kicker: the product demo was set up outside.

In Phoenix.

In August.

On that particular day, it was 118 degrees.

After losing what felt like twenty pounds in sweat, we finally escaped back into the life-saving air-conditioning. I sat in my VP Stacie's office and said, half joking but mostly annoyed:

"I can't believe I had to go to that meeting. Who schedules a product demo at 1:00 p.m., outside, in August . . . in Phoenix!?"

Stacie looked at me, paused, and said:

"It's your fault for being available."

Ouch.

I wanted to complain more, but she was right.

The following week, I made sure that would never happen again. I blocked off as much of my time as possible to focus on what mattered. I created calendar holds for where I was going to be, who I was going to be coaching, why I chose them (based on intel from chapter 4), and what the goal of each coaching session was.

Here is what one day of that looked like:

8:00 a.m.–8:30 a.m.

- Who/Where: Self (office)

- What: Prep and review notes for today's coaching sessions
- Why: Set coaching intentions, review sales performance reports, and identify key focus areas for each salesperson

8:30 a.m.–9:30 a.m.

- Who/Where: Debrief with Stacie and Jennifer from Marketing
- What: Talk about signage at struggling communities and potentially adding a human directional
- Why: Traffic has slowed down, and we are behind plan

10:00 a.m.–11:00 a.m.

- Who/Where: Brian at Pinecrest Model Home
- What: Coaching on closing during the first visit
- Why: Brian's first-visit conversion rate is below target, and the community is off plan

11:30 a.m.–12:30 p.m.

- Who/Where: Debrief with Jennifer and Parker at Tarrington Place
- What: Small group role-play. Specifically handling the "We're just starting to look" objection

- Why: Intel shows this is the most common objection the team is hearing this week

12:30 p.m.–1:00 p.m.

- Who/Where: Lunch (blocked)
- What: Admin time, email catch-up, notes review
- Why: Document coaching notes while fresh and stay connected with leadership

1:30 p.m.–2:15 p.m.

- Who/Where: One-on-one with Marcus at the Meadows
- What: Coaching on effective demonstration and tour flow
- Why: Marcus tends to feature dump and loses momentum mid-tour

2:30 p.m.–3:00 p.m.

- Who/Where: Corporate conference call
- What: Listen to corporate initiatives
- Why: Because I was told I had to be on it ☺

3:30 p.m.–4:15 p.m.

- Who/Where: Team huddle at central office
- What: Large group coaching. Review of current traffic-to-sale ratios across all communities
- Why: Reinforce the importance of follow-up and setting second appointments

4:00 p.m.–4:30 p.m.

- Who/Where: Self (office)
- What: End-of-day reflection and plan for tomorrow
- Why: Review coaching impact from today, update notes, and block time for next week's sessions

You're probably wondering if I stuck to the calendar 100 percent of the time. The honest answer is no. Things come up. Priorities shift. Sometimes your boss has a fire drill, and you have to adjust.

But that's not the point. The point is that you have a plan.

Here's what I did to make sure my plan stuck as often as possible: Every Monday morning, I printed two copies of my calendar. One copy went to my VP of sales. The other went to my division president. I wasn't doing this for them; I was doing it for me. I knew I was going to need backup!

When a random meeting popped up, or someone tried to pull me into something outside of my priorities, I could confidently say: "I've already committed to Stacie and Greg that this time is blocked off for coaching the team."

It worked like a charm.

A day like this isn't reactive. It's designed. When you preplan your calendar, you control your time, your team's growth, and ultimately, your results.

Incorrect Prioritization

Sometimes the person who's messing up your calendar isn't another department or your boss. It's you.

Maybe you've convinced yourself that your job isn't really to coach people. If that's the case, I'm not sure why you're still reading this book! Maybe your boss made you read it? #sorrynotsorry

Most of the time, incorrect prioritization shows up as "I'll get to it after I do . . ." thinking.

It's the idea that you'll coach once you finish the report, once you respond to all the emails, once you deal with the latest fire drill. But coaching doesn't happen *after* the work; it *is* the work.

It's no different from saving money. My son-in-law, Zach Nelson, is a financial coach. And like Dave Ramsey and most financial experts advise, one of Zach's first lessons is to pay yourself first. Why? Because if you try to save after you've paid all the bills, there's usually nothing left . . . and you'll stay broke.

Your time works the same way.

You can't do pipeline impact calls, coaching, and intel gathering after all the meetings are over. Why? Because there will be nothing left.

If coaching isn't the first priority on your calendar, it just won't happen.

Calendar Tips

When I finally learned how to use my calendar as a true productivity tool, my life changed. And here's the truth: The busier you get, the more calendar discipline you need.

Recently, I was on a flight scrolling through my calendar in the thirty-day view. The woman sitting next to me kept glancing at my screen. Eventually, she couldn't help herself; she leaned over and asked, "What on earth do you do?"

She asked because my calendar was completely time blocked and color-coded. To her, it probably looked like Crayola commissioned it as a modern art piece. Every day was filled with intentional activity, and each category had a different color.

That's not an accident. That's how I run my life.

If you're not using this system yet, I'd encourage you to start. Here's why:

When you color-code and time block your calendar, you can instantly see where you're in balance and where you're not. You'll know at a glance if you're spending enough time coaching your team, developing yourself, and spending time with your family, or if you're drowning in meetings.

Now, I'm not going to get into the weeds on how to integrate Gmail with Outlook or set up color tags in Google Calendar. You can find all that on YouTube in about five seconds.

But I am going to stress the importance of creating your own color-coding system.

Personally, I combine my personal and professional calendars in one place so I can see my life as a whole. That way, I'm not just managing my work; I'm managing my time.

Here are some categories you might consider for setting up your system:

> If you don't have a plan for your life, someone else does.

Sample Calendar Color-Coding Categories

- Green: Coaching sessions (one-on-one, small group, large group)
- Blue: Pipeline Impact Calls and intel gathering
- Yellow: Meetings and administrative tasks (division meetings, reports, sales rally planning)
- Red: Revenue-generating activities (strategy sessions, pricing meetings, key sales calls)
- Orange: Personal development (reading, webinars, training events)
- Purple: Personal life (family time, vacations, health appointments, date nights)
- Gray: Buffer time (email catch-up, travel, commute, margin in your day)
- Teal: Prep and reflection (planning coaching sessions, end-of-week review)

This system allows you to look at your calendar and immediately understand where your time is going and where it needs to go next.

Remember: If you don't have a plan for your life, someone else does.

Summary

Coaching doesn't happen by accident; it happens by appointment. If you don't intentionally block time for coaching, follow-up, and intel gathering, you'll default to the urgent instead of the important. Meetings, reports, and random requests will flood your calendar and steal time away from what actually drives revenue: helping your sales team improve. It's not about working harder; it's about working on the right things.

Your calendar is a reflection of your true priorities. When you color-code it, time block it, and share it with your leadership team, you create accountability for where your focus should be. Coaching your team isn't extra work . . . it is the work. When you master your calendar, you don't just control your time; you control your impact.

Questions to Ponder

- What percentage of your current calendar is dedicated to coaching and team development?
- Where are you allowing other departments or tasks to hijack your time?
- If someone looked at your calendar today, would they be able to tell that coaching your team is one of your top priorities?

CHAPTER FIFTEEN

COACHING WHEN IT'S HARD: THE FOUR TOUGHEST PROFILES AND THE FOUR TOUGHEST SCENARIOS

It's supposed to be hard. If it wasn't hard, everyone would do it. The hard is what makes it great.

—Jimmy Dugan (*A League of Their Own*)

Throughout this book, I've shared a few stories of difficult coaching scenarios—some I've experienced personally, others I've helped leaders navigate. Until now, I haven't defined exactly what makes a coaching situation difficult. In this chapter, we'll look at four tough profiles and four of the toughest coaching moments that consistently challenge even the most seasoned leaders.

The Four Toughest Profiles

In chapter 5, I introduced the two critical traits to prioritize when adding someone to your team:

- Coachability
- Drive

To reinforce why these two traits matter so much, consider this: Every one of the tough coaching profiles you're about to read about struggles with either coachability, drive, or both. That's what makes them hard to lead . . . and exactly why this chapter matters.

The Know-It-All

You know the type. Years of experience, has all the answers, and has absolutely zero interest in being coached. Why? Because they already know everything! I touched on this briefly with the story of Chelsea, the sales manager in chapter 5 who was told by Nick, "Sweetheart, I've been doing this for thirty years. I know what I'm doing."

Nick is a classic Know-It-All.

The real question is this: Can someone like Nick actually be coached? To answer that, we have to understand why someone becomes a Know-It-All in the first place. It usually comes down to one of two reasons:

1. They're afraid of being told they're wrong or not measuring up.
2. Their ego is so inflated they genuinely believe they have nothing left to learn.

The first type can be coached. But it requires you to break through their fear and show them that coaching isn't about criticism, it's about support and growth.

Put yourself in their shoes for a moment. They've been doing the job for fifteen or twenty years, and now someone new is telling them they're doing it wrong. That's a tough pill to swallow, even for the best veterans.

You probably already know who the Know-It-All is on your team, but just in case, here are a few common tells:

- They talk over you, interrupt you, or constantly correct you.
- They use phrases like "This doesn't apply to me," or "I've been doing this a long time."
- They reject feedback . . . unless it confirms what they already believe.

Many sales leaders handle this profile the wrong way. They get pulled into a battle of egos, which never ends well. Or worse, they avoid coaching the person entirely.

If the behavior is rooted in fear, your job is to win them over, not overpower them. But if they truly believe they're beyond coaching, then you have a more serious issue.

And that leads to a hard question:

Are you willing to keep someone on your team who is uncoachable?

The Time-Waster

This one might be the most frustrating of all coaching profiles because on the surface, they seem totally coachable. They nod, they smile, they say all the right things. They even ask great questions about how to improve, which makes you think they're all in.

But then . . . nothing changes.

Week after week, they come back with the same challenges, the same missed expectations, and the same lack of execution. You start to feel like you're on a coaching treadmill, doing a lot of work but going nowhere.

The reason this profile is so challenging is because they *look* coachable. They've learned the language of growth, but they haven't embraced the discipline of change. In truth, they don't need more advice; they need to do something with the advice they've already been given.

So what's really going on?

There are a few possibilities:

- They don't want to disappoint you, so they fake buy-in instead of admitting confusion or disinterest.
- They're overwhelmed and don't know how to take the first step, so they hide behind questions.
- Or they're addicted to the idea of getting better but unwilling to endure the discomfort required to actually improve.

The challenge for you as a coach is not to confuse engagement with progress. You have to measure what matters, and that means verifying actual behavior change. Conversations don't count. Performance improvement does.

Here's how to spot the Time Waster:

- They agree while you are coaching them but never actually follow through or implement the coaching.
- They frequently seek more "clarity," but use it as a way to avoid the work.
- You find yourself repeating the same advice over and over with no change in behavior.

To coach this person well, you have to change your strategy:

- Set short, specific action items and follow up like crazy.
- Ask them to demonstrate, not just talk.
- Celebrate follow-through more than insight.

- And if progress flatlines, be direct: "We've had some great conversations. Now I need to see it in action."

At some point, you have to decide: Are you coaching someone who's actually trying or someone who's wasting your time?

The Constant Underperformer

There are times when you have to call it what it is. If you've coached someone consistently, poured time and energy into their development, and the results still aren't there, then you may be dealing with a Constant Underperformer.

This is the person who genuinely wants to succeed. They're open to coaching, eager to learn, and even take initiative, and maybe they've reached out to the sales trainer on their own, signed up for extra sessions, or volunteered to shadow a top performer. Their attitude isn't the problem. But despite all that, they just can't seem to put it together.

This is where leadership gets difficult. Because it's easy to cut ties with someone who's toxic or resistant. But this person is actually trying. They're probably really nice. They're *almost* there. And that almost can make you keep trying for too long.

As my wife wisely says, "If you choose to do one thing, you are choosing not to do something else in that same moment." Every week you spend hoping this person will turn the corner is a week you're not investing in someone who can.

Odds are, at some point, you'll need to make the call to move on. That's not failure; it's called leadership. You gave them every chance. You took their performance skills as far as they would go. You led with heart and with action. But sometimes, the best support you can give someone is to let them find a role where they're better suited to succeed.

And in doing that, you create space for someone who will get results.

The Victim

The Victim is, without question, one of the most exhausting salespeople to coach. And I say that with full empathy because I used to be this person.

Back in my early days, nothing was ever my fault. If I lost a sale, I had a dozen reasons ready to go: It was my competitor's shady tactics, my sales partner's mistake, the supplier's delay, bad leads (I mean, where were the Glengarry leads when I needed them?), or of course . . . my manager just didn't understand.

The trademark of the Victim is external blame. They're constantly pointing outward instead of looking inward. They believe their situation is unique, unfair, and unsolvable, which makes coaching feel like pushing a rope up a hill.

The question is: Can the Victim be coached? The answer is yes (I am proof). They need a leader who refuses to enable the excuses and helps them take responsibility.

In order to coach them, you have to shift their focus from what's out of their control to what's in their control. You have to challenge their thinking without triggering defensiveness. And most of all, you have to be patient. Victims don't change overnight. It often takes small wins before accountability shows up.

Underneath the Victim story is usually a talented person who's simply afraid of failing or afraid of owning the result. That certainly was true for me. Your job is to help them see that success doesn't come from perfection. It comes from taking a position of progress, not perfection.

The Four Toughest Coaching Moments

After two decades of coaching salespeople, I can tell you without hesitation, coaching can be tough.

In 2023, I was in Raleigh, North Carolina, leading a two-day sales-training event. Day one was focused on overcoming objections. Day two was designed for hands-on, small group coaching. It's a high-touch, practical day where we get into the tactical details of real selling moments.

During one of the practice rounds, I observed a salesperson named Rachel working through an objection. As always, I had set the tone for a safe and supportive coaching environment.

When Rachel finished her practice session, I asked if I could share some insight. She agreed, but her tone said otherwise. Still, I gently pointed out that her body language had shifted into a defensive posture when responding to the objection. I encouraged her to relax more physically as she delivered the strategy, so her presence would better support her words.

That was when it happened.

Rachel cut me off mid-sentence and snapped, "This is a bunch of BS. I know how to overcome objections, for crying out loud. This is a waste of my time!"

I'll be honest . . . My first instinct was to punch back. But I didn't.

Instead, I stayed calm and said, "I get it. Practice can feel fake sometimes. It can even feel like someone's telling you that you don't know what you're doing. That's not what I'm saying. I'm saying that if you're open to it, I can help you take your results to another level. Are you open to that?"

What do you think Rachel did?

If you think Rachel calmed down and continued with the session, you'd be wrong. She turned to me and said, "I can't do this. This isn't reality." Then she grabbed her purse, stormed out of the training, got in her car, and literally drove away.

The reality is you can't control how people respond to coaching. You can only control how you show up as a coach.

After the session, I spent some time reflecting on how I'd handled it. I played it back, wondering if I could have done anything differently. In the end, I believe I handled it right. I wasn't harsh, I didn't overstep, and I even asked permission to coach. The truth is, Rachel wasn't going to engage in coaching, no matter who the coach was or how many soft skills they deployed.

That moment reminded me of something important: It's not just the tough people that make coaching hard. It's the tough moments . . . the emotional, unpredictable, high-pressure situations that test your patience, your professionalism, and your commitment to leading with grace.

With that in mind, let's take a look at four of the toughest coaching moments you're likely to face and how to handle them when they happen.

Moment #1: The Walkout

I've had this happen to me a handful of times in my coaching career. I'd love to tell you that at some point it stops bothering you, but that would be a lie. When it happens, it can rattle you. If you're not careful, it can even make you shy away from coaching altogether, especially if the salesperson makes a scene in front of others.

The key is twofold: Do your best to avoid it and know how to recover when it happens.

How to Avoid This Situation

Most of the time, you can spot a potential "walkout" candidate before it happens. But sometimes, it will still catch you off guard. Avoiding it starts with making sure the coaching environment is safe. Pick a place where the salesperson won't feel embarrassed, attacked, or put on the spot before they're ready.

Your best defense in these situations is using encouragement, empathy, and curiosity to keep the conversation safe and productive.

I've been able to steer plenty of people away from a meltdown simply by slowing things down and meeting them where they were emotionally. To do that, first watch for the early warning signs: They start to get flustered, their tone sharpens, their pace speeds up. When you notice it, ease off. Pause. Take a short break. In some cases, it's better to stop the session altogether and reschedule. That kind of pattern interrupt can keep a tense moment from turning into a full-on walkout.

How to Recover When a Walkout Happens

If they do walk out and you couldn't prevent it, the worst thing you can do is chase them down or demand they come back. They likely need space. If you're in a public setting, it's often better for a peer to check in on them rather than you. Later, when emotions have cooled down, you can follow up privately. You want to keep the tone professional and calm, with the focus on moving forward and helping improve their performance.

In the times when this has happened to me, I will reconnect with the individual and simply check on them by asking how they are doing. Sometimes you learn that there is something going on personally that caused the walkout and it had nothing to do with you, the practice session, the content, or work at all.

The walkout doesn't have to derail your coaching long-term. It only becomes a lasting problem if you let the fear of it stop you from having the conversations your team needs to grow.

Moment #2: The Emotional Overload

Years ago, I was coaching a salesperson named Erica. She had been one of our most consistent top performers and was always in the top five. Then, seemingly overnight, she fell off the map. She couldn't close a door, as the saying goes.

Naturally, I scheduled a coaching session to focus on asking for the sale. A recent mystery shop had shown that she'd stopped asking buyers to commit altogether. In my mind, this was an easy fix.

I couldn't have been more wrong.

From the moment the session started, I could tell something was off. Erica was going through the motions, but her mind was somewhere else. This wasn't the bold, driven bulldog we had hired. In her interview, she'd closed us by asking when she could start!

I paused the coaching and simply asked, "Are you doing okay?"

That's all it took.

Erica looked at me, her eyes welled up, and she broke down in tears. I'll be honest—handling moments like that doesn't come naturally to me. But I knew enough to stay present. I didn't rush to solve anything. I just sat with her and asked what was going on.

She wiped her eyes and said, "Well . . . my father is back in my life. He abandoned our family when I was a kid. Now he's staying at my house, and it's really hard."

As she opened up more, the full story came out. When she was little, every time she asked her father for anything—a toy, attention, help—he would often respond with physical abuse.

And just like that, her lack of closing made complete sense.

You and I likely aren't trained therapists. But sometimes, coaching puts us in deeply human moments that require the same skills: asking good questions, listening without judgment, and holding space for someone to be vulnerable. That's what I did with Erica. I let her talk. I let her feel.

When the emotions subsided, I helped her to reframe what "asking for the sale" meant. For Erica, the act of asking had become unconsciously linked to danger. The internal wiring said:

Ask = Abuse

Together, we built a new frame: Asking for the sale is not a threat; it's a gift. I told her, "You're not pushing people. You're offering to help them improve their lives. That's what we sell—life improvement. When you ask for the sale, you're asking if they want your help."

It didn't click overnight. But over time, Erica found her way back. She regained her confidence. And her results followed.

The key to the emotional-overload moment is presence. Don't rush it. Don't fix it. Stay calm. Listen. Let the emotion pass, and when the time is right, bring the conversation back to belief, growth, and possibility.

What I have come to realize is that sometimes, the breakthrough a salesperson needs isn't about skill development. It's about showing that you care about the person beyond the sale.

Moment #3: You're Coaching a Former Peer

Many of you reading this were promoted from the sales floor. That's awesome. And it comes with some built-in challenges. Suddenly, you're managing the very people you used to go to lunch with . . . and maybe even talk a little smack about leadership. Now you are the leadership.

When this shift happens, the dynamic changes whether you like it or not. You can't coach someone effectively if they still see you as "one of them." You have to redefine the relationship.

I've been in that role myself, and I've coached many new sales leaders through it. The best advice I can give is to set new boundaries and expectations before you find yourself in a difficult coaching moment. If you've already stepped into the role, it's not too late. But you'll need to reset the relationship clearly and directly.

It might sound something like this:

> "I've always respected the way we've worked together. And I want you to know I'm still here to support you. That said,

Relationships are built on agreements.

my role has changed, and so has our dynamic. I'm now responsible for helping you grow, and that means I may need to challenge you or hold you accountable in ways I didn't before. That doesn't change how I feel about you, but it does change how we work together. Does that make sense?"

This kind of conversation doesn't need to be dramatic. In fact, the more confident and natural you are, the more likely they'll respect the boundary. Don't overapologize for the shift. Step into your leadership fully, and lead with clarity, care, and consistency.

The moment you become the coach, your job isn't to preserve old friendships. It's to help your team reach new levels of performance.

As I like to say, relationships are built on agreements.

Moment #4: You're Off as the Coach

Sometimes, you're just not on your A game. It happens. You're human.

Maybe something's going on at home that's weighing on you. Maybe you just got off a tough call with your senior VP, who let you know you're not meeting expectations. And right after that, you walk straight into a coaching session.

There are a few hidden dangers in this moment.

First, you're more likely to be emotionally reactive and could get triggered by something small and make it bigger than it needs to be. Second, you're not fully present, which can come across as disinterest or detachment. Third, you're more vulnerable to being thrown off your game, especially by a Time Waster or a Know-It-All. In that state, you may let things slide that you normally wouldn't, or you may snap in a way that damages trust.

There are two healthy ways to handle this:

1. **Use a Precoaching Reset**

    Before you step into a session, take five minutes to get centered. Close your laptop. Put your phone away. Take a breath. Remind yourself of the purpose of the session and what success looks like. It doesn't take long, but it makes a huge difference.

2. **Reschedule if You Have To**

    If you know you're not in a place to be the best coach possible, don't fake it. It's better to delay than to show up half present and do damage. You might say,

"Hey, John, are you open to rescheduling our session to tomorrow? I want to give you my full attention because this coaching matters, and unfortunately, something has come up."

The bottom line is this: If you're off, own it. Reset or reschedule. Coaching is too important to phone in. Start to model that kind of self-awareness and give your team permission to lead themselves the same way.

Tough coaching moments will test your patience, your confidence, and sometimes even your desire to keep showing up. But these are also the moments that shape your leadership the most. If you can stay steady when things get emotional, uncomfortable, or unpredictable, you'll become the kind of coach people trust even when the work is hard.

Summary

Coaching is rarely perfect. It's often tough, emotional, and deeply human. The goal isn't to control every outcome but to show up with intention, awareness, and a commitment to growth for yourself and the person you're leading. When things feel messy or uncomfortable, it doesn't mean you're doing it wrong. It often means you're exactly where you need to be.

What separates great coaches from good ones isn't how they lead when it's easy . . . It's how they respond when it's not. Stay present. Stay clear. Stay anchored in your purpose. That's where the transformation happens.

Questions to Ponder

- Which coaching profile do you find most challenging, and why?
- How do you typically react when a coaching moment goes sideways?
- What can you do to prepare yourself emotionally and mentally for tough coaching moments?

CHAPTER SIXTEEN

COACHING SOUNDS GOOD, BUT . . .

If it's important to you, you'll find a way.
If not, you'll find an excuse.

—Jim Rohn

I probably should have made this the first chapter of the book. I say that because odds are fairly high that if you've made it this far, you've likely bought in to what I've been saying. And . . . you still might have some reasons why you either can't coach or why you shouldn't coach.

Allow this chapter to be my tough conversation with you on why you must coach your team.

Years ago, I worked for a Fortune 500 home builder as a sales leader. I had a great desk in a cushy office building with coffee makers, a stocked fridge, and a lot of peers I considered friends. It was comfortable, familiar, and easy to stay behind the glass walls.

Then one Saturday, everything changed.

Marcia Dillon, our senior VP of sales, walked into the empty office with a stack of U-Haul boxes and a mission. Marcia was a brilliant leader from Louisiana with a sharp wit, unmatched instincts, and a no-nonsense approach to performance. She had started her home-building career in Dallas (on the construction side, no less) and worked her way up through grit, results, and an uncanny ability to see through excuses. To this day, she's one of my heroes. I wouldn't be where I am without her.

That morning, Marcia boxed up our desks . . . mine and all the other sales managers'. She sent our things to the field. In our company, we had a central division office, and we had communities scattered across the Phoenix valley. That was where the salespeople worked. That was where the coaching needed to happen.

She gathered the managers together and said, "Your job is to coach the team, and you can't do that from behind a desk. As of today, you're no longer allowed in this office unless we're having a sales rally or a manager meeting."

Marcia didn't just move our stuff; she shattered every excuse we had for not showing up where we were needed. So before we go into the reasons sales leaders often give for not coaching, just know this: I've had them too. I've said them. I've believed them. But I've also had someone who called me out. Now it's my turn to do the same for you.

Here are the top reasons sales leaders don't coach and my response to each of them.

1. I Don't Have Time to Coach

I recall when I met my wife, Melissa. I had just released my first book, *The Sales Cure*, and was travelling the country doing trainings all across the US. Melissa lived in Albuquerque, and I lived in Phoenix. Logically, it made no sense to date someone who lived in the one state I didn't travel to. And . . . I am pretty sure there were women in Phoenix I could have dated. I didn't have time for a relationship, let alone a long-distance relationship. And then I met her.

You can probably see where this is going.

All of a sudden, I find myself making time. Where I once had zero time, I am now on the phone every night for three hours saying things like, "No, you hang up first."

The point is that we make time for whatever is important to us. You likely have time to coach; it just isn't a priority to you yet. Hopefully, after you read this book, that will change. The only other reason you might say you don't have time is because you're stuck in a bunch of meetings. I will handle that one in a minute.

The bottom line is you have to make the time, and you have to prioritize it on your calendar. Go back and reread chapter 14. Start time blocking coaching sessions and use a color-coding system to help you see where your priorities might be out of order.

2. My Manager/President/Company Owner Wants Me in Meetings All the Time

This one's tough.

On one hand, your boss is telling you that your presence is required in back-to-back meetings. On the other, you've come to understand that coaching your team is not just part of your job . . . It's the highest and best use of your time. (If you don't know this at this point in the book, I recommend starting over. ☺)

If you're caught in this tug-of-war, don't lose hope. But also, don't expect it to fix itself. This is an opportunity to lead up.

A great way to approach this scenario is to treat it like a sales challenge. Your "buyer" is your boss, and your "product" is the performance improvement that comes from you coaching your people consistently. Your job now is to help your leadership team see that spending hours in meetings, while sometimes necessary, doesn't drive revenue the way skill development does. Show them what happens when you invest in your team. Track it. Document it. Share stories of improvement and wins that came directly from coaching moments.

This isn't about rebellion; it's about reframing priorities. Your leaders don't want your calendar full—they want results. Coaching delivers those results. Make that case clearly, consistently, and with data to back it up.

One idea is to get your leadership team to read this book! #jokingnotjoking

3. Our Company Has a Trainer

It's great that your company has a trainer. That tells me they value growth and development, which is a good thing. But using that as a reason not to coach your team is like a father saying, "Well, the kids have a mother, so I don't need to be involved." You wouldn't say that as a parent, and you shouldn't say it as a leader either.

Odds are high that you spend far more time with your sales team than the company trainer does. Most trainers are focused on onboarding, systems, sales meetings, and one-off events, not on sustained, in-the-field performance improvement. Their role is important, but it's not the same as yours.

Coaching is about reinforcement, accountability, and the kind of development that only comes from ongoing connection. Remember, management isn't the direction of people . . . It's the development of them. And no one is better positioned to do that than you.

Even with the best trainer in the business, your team still needs you.

4. We Have an Outside Trainer

Sometimes companies bring in outside trainers to develop their sales team. I know because I am that trainer.

Outside trainers can bring fresh energy, new techniques, and expanded perspectives. We can introduce mindset shifts, skill upgrades, and best practices from across the industry. And in many cases, we do help spark improvement. But here's the truth: No outside trainer, no matter how good, can create lasting transformation without consistent coaching from you.

Real change doesn't happen in the classroom. It happens in the follow-up. In the repetition. In the coaching conversations and activities that happen day in and day out.

When I work with sales teams, I also train the sales leaders on the 4E Coaching Method and hold them accountable to keep the momentum going long after the workshop ends. A great training session is only the beginning. Habit change takes time, support, and leadership.

So yes, bring in the outside help. But don't outsource your responsibility. Your team still needs your voice, your eyes, and your guidance to lock in the training to make it a new habit.

5. I Have an Experienced Team

This might be one of the most common reasons sales leaders give for not coaching their team. I often hear things like, "I only hire experienced people so I don't have to coach." On one hand, I get it. It sounds efficient. Less training, less hand-holding, less time investment.

But in reality? That mindset brings a whole different set of problems.

The first question you have to ask is: Where did that experience come from? If you have a team of fifteen experienced sales professionals, chances are they were trained by fifteen different companies, coached by fifteen different leaders, and formed habits in fifteen different ways. That means inconsistency. Inconsistency in your process, in your systems, and most importantly, in your customer experience.

And let's not forget Nick, the guy with thirty years of experience that turned out to be one year of experience repeated thirty times.

Hiring experienced people isn't a bad thing. But experience doesn't guarantee excellence. It doesn't guarantee alignment. And it definitely doesn't guarantee coachability.

Every person on your team, no matter how seasoned, needs coaching. Don't confuse years on the résumé with mastery in the role. Experience might get them in the door, but your coaching is what moves them toward mastery.

6. My Team Is More Experienced Than Me

I can totally relate to this one. I became a sales leader at the ripe age of twenty-nine. In fact, when I was interviewed by Steve, the division president, he voiced a very real concern: Some of the sales team had been selling longer than I'd been alive.

To be fair, he had a point.

But I was hungry. I believed I had something to offer. I told him I wasn't coming in to be the expert with all the answers. My plan was to lean into the experience on the team, especially the veterans, and I was going to use them as part of the coaching strategy and give them credit when it made sense. That way, the coaching didn't feel like it was coming from me; it felt like it was coming from the team. He loved the answer, and I got the job.

You don't need to be the most experienced person in the room to be an effective coach. Coaching isn't about knowing everything; it's about helping your team reach new levels of performance.

Remember the story of Michael Phelps from chapter 3?

Phelps is the most decorated Olympian of all time. No one has spent more time in the water, and no one has won more gold. But even at the height of his career, he had a coach, Bob Bowman. Bowman wasn't a better swimmer than Phelps. He didn't need to be. His genius wasn't in beating Phelps—it was in *seeing* Phelps. Coaching him. Pushing him. Guiding him to become even greater.

If Michael Phelps needs a coach, so does your team. And you don't have to outswim them to lead them.

Coaching isn't something you do because sales are bad. It's something you do so sales stay good.

7. We're Making Sales

This one is so common it's almost expected.

Even when a sales leader starts strong, getting into the rhythm of regular coaching, success can quickly become the very thing that derails it. The team starts hitting their numbers, momentum picks up, and suddenly the one-on-ones get pushed. Your calendar, once filled with coaching sessions, is now back-to-back meetings and "urgent" admin tasks. The thinking is often "We're doing well. I can ease up a bit."

Trust me when I tell you . . . It's a trap!

Coaching isn't something you do *because* sales are bad. It's something you do so sales stay good.

When things are going well, coaching is easier, more energizing, and frankly, more enjoyable. That's when your people are open. That's when confidence is high. And that's when you have the greatest chance to fine-tune the little details that separate good from great.

Remember, coaching isn't a fire drill. It's a daily discipline. It's the reason you're selling, not an activity for when you're not.

If you only coach when things are falling apart, you're not building a high-performing team; you're just reacting. Coaching should be as permanent in your calendar as payroll.

8. I'm Not a Very Good Coach

Well, it's a good thing you're reading this book!

Seriously, though, most sales leaders aren't taught how to coach. They're promoted for their sales performance, handed a team, and expected to figure it out as they go. There's no Coaching 101 built into most management onboarding programs. Coaching is a learned skill, and like anything else, you have to want to learn it.

I've personally invested hundreds of thousands of dollars into seminars, courses, mentorship, and professional development . . . including learning how to coach. Why? Because I believe coaching is one of the most powerful levers a leader can pull.

But here's what I want you to remember: Your current skill level should never be the reason you don't coach. My first few coaching sessions? Total train wrecks. I stumbled. I fumbled. They were awkward and unclear, and I probably confused people more than I helped them. But I didn't let that stop me. I used those early experiences as fuel to get better.

You don't have to be world class right now. You just have to care enough to start and be committed enough to keep going.

And if you want structured support, I've built an entire yearlong coaching certification program that teaches sales leaders how to coach using the 4E Coaching Method. You can find more details and resources at **RevenueGetter.com**.

Coaching is a skill. And skills can be learned.

Summary

Every sales leader has a reason why they can't coach or shouldn't coach. Some of them even sound legitimate. You've got meetings. You've got a trainer. You've got a seasoned team. Or maybe you just don't feel all that confident in your coaching skills. I've heard them all, and I've used a few of them myself.

If coaching really is the most important thing you can do as a leader (and it is), then no excuse holds water. Not one. Coaching isn't a reward for free time. It's the reason your team grows. It's the reason performance improves. And it's the reason you have a job in the first place. This chapter wasn't written to make you feel bad. It was written to help you call it like it is, move past the excuses, and step fully into your role as a developer of people.

Questions to Ponder

- Which excuse in this chapter hit closest to home and why?
- What would your calendar say about your real priorities as a leader?
- If nothing changed from here, what would your team miss out on?

CHAPTER SEVENTEEN

FROM READING TO REVENUE

Your future is whatever you make of it, so make it a good one.

—Doc Brown (*Back to the Future*)

In the summer of 2024, I was at the top of my game. I was part of the largest coaching and training company in my industry. My calendar was full, my income was the highest it had ever been, and my clients loved me. I could have easily stayed there until the end of my career. And at fifty years old, I had no plans to leave.

But if I'm being honest, something was missing.

My wife had been encouraging me for years to go out on my own. I always brushed her suggestion off, mostly because I was comfortable. Then, right after a massive annual event our company put on, someone (other than my wife) told me I should go out on my own. The next day, someone else said the exact same words. Over the next three weeks, three more people told me the same thing.

For those who know me, I'm not a wild risk taker. I'm fairly conservative and like a solid plan before I make a move. I even send meeting invites to my wife for date nights, as I mentioned earlier.

I won't go into all the details, but I had a moment where I prayed about the decision. Should I stay, or should I go? (As the Clash famously asked.) The answer was clear: I needed to go. Still, it was scary. I would have no guaranteed income, no safety net, no clear road map.

I called Lindsey Ayala, now the chief growth officer at Impact Eighty-Eight, and told her what I was thinking. I said that if I did take the leap, I'd want her on board with me. Lindsey was between jobs and on the verge of making another move when I called. She listened and then asked, in her straightforward Southern accent, "Ryan, how sure are you that you're going to do this?"

"I'm about 70 percent sure," I said.

Without missing a beat, she replied, "Well . . . you better get to 100 percent if you want me to do this."

In that moment, I knew I had to commit or walk away. I could either cling to what was safe or step into what was possible.

Every leader eventually stands at that same crossroads . . . the place where comfort and calling meet. One path keeps you where you are, surrounded by the familiar, getting the same results you've always gotten. The other leads into the unknown, filled with risk, stretch, and the potential to do something bigger than you've ever done before.

You're at that place right now. The pages behind you are knowledge. The pages ahead of you are blank. What you write next is entirely up to you.

My prayer for you is that you choose to take the leap from sales manager to RevenueGetter.

The RevenueGetter Playbook

I want you to hit the ground running, so I've built a three-tier action plan to get you moving.

- Immediate actions
- Thirty-day actions
- Ongoing habits

You can also download a checklist at **RevenueGetter.com/tools.**

Immediate Actions (Next Forty-Eight Hours)

1. **Analyze Your Team, Person by Person**

   Do a complete, honest assessment of each salesperson. Who's winning? Who's struggling? Who takes every sale as far as it can go . . . and who's just mailing it in? Get clear on exactly what you're dealing with so you can coach from reality, not assumption.

2. **Schedule Your Next (or First) 4E Coaching Session**

   Don't overthink it—just book it. The longer you wait, the more likely this book turns into "shelf-help." Put it on the calendar now.

3. **Identify One Sales Skill to Focus on This Week**

   Go back to chapter 4 and decide on a single skill to improve. One clear focus drives faster action and deeper results than trying to fix everything at once.

4. **Have a One-on-One About Their "Why"**

   Sit down with at least one team member and uncover their personal motivation for being in sales. Remember: You're coaching for their goals, not yours. The sooner you start these conversations, the stronger your coaching will be.

Thirty-Day Actions

5. **Create Your Quarterly Coaching Calendar**

   Map out your coaching sessions for the next three months. Include who you'll coach, when, and on what skill. A plan beats "I'll get to it when I can" every time.

6. **Implement a Verification Plan for One Key Skill**

   Pick one skill your team needs to master and set up checkpoints to verify progress. Do some observation, role-plays, mystery shops . . . whatever it takes. Remember that trust is nice, but verification is where the truth lives.

7. **Run a Follow-Up Audit**

   Review every active prospect in your CRM. Is each one being followed up with the right frequency and method? Eliminate gaps before they become lost sales.

8. **Celebrate a Win Publicly**

Highlight one achievement (big or small) in front of the whole team. Recognition fuels performance and reinforces the behaviors you want repeated.

Ongoing Habits

9. **Hold Weekly Pipeline Impact Calls**

Review each salesperson's pipeline, not as a punishment but as a chance to ask questions, uncover opportunities, and remove obstacles. Listen for coaching opportunities and where your team might be stuck.

10. **Track and Celebrate Behaviors**

Don't just celebrate sales. Celebrate the behaviors that lead to those sales. Did someone send out a video follow-up? Did someone start asking for the sale? Did a salesperson stop twitching when they quote price? Great! Shout it from the rooftops. Remember, what gets recognized gets repeated.

11. **Stay Connected to the Sales Floor**

Don't let your role pull you so far into reports and meetings that you lose touch with the action. Spend time observing presentations, greeting buyers, and feeling the pulse of your market firsthand.

12. **Model the Behaviors You Want Your Team to Adopt**

    Show up early, prepare thoroughly, follow up relentlessly. Whatever you want from your team, let them see you living it. Leadership is contagious; make sure they're catching the right things.

Your Personal Development Plan

In my entire career, I've never been handed a formal development plan. Not once. Every plan I've ever had, I built myself and then asked for the support I needed to achieve it.

That said, I was fortunate enough to get one piece of advice from a mentor that completely shaped how I approached growth. He told me there were three areas I needed to focus on if I wanted to keep developing my skills. Those three areas have stuck with me to this day, and I want to share them with you in the hope they inspire you to grow beyond the pages of this book.

1. **Associate Up**

    Spend time with people who are ahead of you in skill, mindset, and results. Surround yourself with high performers who will challenge your thinking and raise your standards. Specifically, find someone who is a great coach and pick their brain. I promise it will pay dividends.

2. **Read Great Books**

   Books are a low-cost, high-return way to sharpen your thinking and expand your perspective. You literally can steal the thoughts and life experiences of people who have achieved what you want to achieve. I would encourage you to read both inside and outside your industry. Read books on leadership, psychology, and sales, as well as biographies and anything else that makes you better.

3. **Listen to Great People**

   Find audio recordings, podcasts, and interviews with people who are already where you want to be. I guarantee you there is a podcast by someone on any topic you want to study. Listen to them and study their habits, learn their stories, and model what works.

Growth doesn't happen by accident. It's a decision and a discipline. Build your plan and work it daily, and you'll be amazed at how far you can go.

I challenge you to create your development plan and stick to it. Not for a week. Not until you get busy. Not until the next fire pops up in your business. Stick to it until it becomes part of who you are as a leader.

My hope is that you adopt a lifetime commitment to learning.

As my father, Jerry Taft, used to say: "Living is learning."

CONCLUSION

In closing, remember that Rome wasn't built in a day. The Sistine Chapel took Michelangelo four years to complete . . . and that was with him working at the highest level of his craft. You don't get into shape after one visit to the gym, and you don't become a master coach after one session. Change is a process, not an event.

Becoming a true RevenueGetter is a journey. There's no shortcut, no quick hack, no "one weird trick" that will instantly transform you. On a scale of one through ten, odds are you won't be a ten out of the gate. Maybe you're starting as a three right now. That's not a problem; it's just your starting point.

If you're a three, aim to become a six. Once you're a six, push to become an eight. Growth is about closing the gap between where you are and where you could be, and that happens through steady, deliberate action.

This is where your development plan becomes your compass. It will keep you pointed in the right direction when the day-to-day grind tries to pull you off course. There will be days when you don't feel like reading the book on your list, making the call to your mentor, or blocking time for coaching. Those are the days when sticking to your plan matters most.

Your development plan is a promise you make to yourself and to your team. By committing to your growth, you're telling them, "I'm not asking you to do anything I'm not willing to do myself." You become the example. You model the mindset. You set the standard.

So start where you are. Build your plan. Work it every day. Give yourself the time and grace to improve, but also hold yourself to a higher standard than you did yesterday. Inch by inch, habit by habit, you'll close the gap between the leader you are now and the leader you're capable of becoming.

RevenueGetters aren't born; they're built. And you've just taken the first step.

I'm eager to hear about your experiences and journey as you work toward becoming a skilled RevenueGetter.

Until then,

Stay hungry!

Ryan Taft

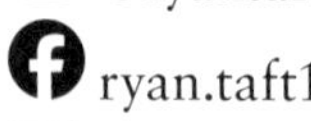

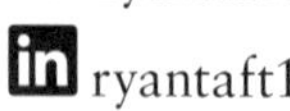

HOW TO WORK WITH RYAN

Thank you for taking the time to read *RevenueGetter* and for investing in your growth as a leader and coach. My goal is that this book has been more than a good read—that it's become a lasting resource to help you lead better conversations, elevate performance, and grow your people.

If you're ready to take the next step, the following are a few ways we can work together. Inquiries can be made at **RevenueGetter.com**. Scan the QR code below to go there now!

1. Book Ryan to Speak

If you're hosting a company event, sales kickoff, or leadership retreat, let's make it unforgettable. Ryan delivers keynote experiences that combine storytelling, data-driven coaching, and humor—designed to shift mindsets and inspire real action. Popular keynotes include:

- RevenueGetter: The Leadership Habits That Drive Sales Results
- People Over Process: Why Your Sales Process Might Be Costing You Sales
- Why Curiosity Is Your Number One Sales Skill

2. Enroll in the RevenueGetter Coaching Certification

This year-long program is designed for sales leaders who want to move beyond management into true performance coaching. You'll master the 4E Coaching Method™, develop real coaching habits, and learn to drive measurable results through behavior change. The program includes:

- Four quarterly intensives with live facilitation
- Peer coaching sessions and video submissions
- RevenueGetter Coaching Certification (upon completion)

3. Attend a Live Event or Workshop

From Speak to Lead (for leaders who want to communicate with confidence) to our Leadership Workshops, each event is designed to sharpen the way you think, speak, and coach.

4. Bring Ryan and His Team to Your Organization

We work with companies across North America to create customized leadership and sales coaching programs that fit your goals, culture, and customer experience. Whether it's developing leaders, improving conversion rates, or strengthening communication, we build programs that drive lasting results.

5. Stay Connected

Get practical insights, stories, and tools to help you coach, communicate, and perform at a higher level. Subscribe to our YouTube channel and connect with us on social media.

- LinkedIn: linkedin.com/in/ryantaft1
- Instagram: @ryantaft
- YouTube: @ImpactEightyEight

If *RevenueGetter* helped you lead with more clarity and purpose, please leave a review on Amazon—your feedback helps others grow too.

ACKNOWLEDGMENTS

Writing a book is never a solo act. It may have my name on the cover, but there is an entire community of people who made *RevenueGetter* possible. I am deeply grateful to each of you.

To the incredible team at Amplify Publishing—Naren Aryal and Brandon Coward—thank you for believing in this project and guiding me through the publishing process. Your professionalism and insight gave me the confidence that this message could reach the leaders who need it most.

To Marcia Dillon: I wouldn't be where I am today without you. Your mentorship, friendship, and faith in me have shaped the trajectory of my career and life. I am forever in your debt.

To our clients at Impact Eighty-Eight—you inspire me daily. Every coaching session, training, and conversation has sharpened my thinking and deepened my conviction that sales leaders have the power to transform lives. Thank you for trusting me with your teams and allowing me to experiment, refine, and share the frameworks found in these pages.

To the gifted team at Insight Picture Co.—Matt Fuller and Ryan Broomberg—you have an uncanny ability to bring ideas to life visually. Your creativity continues to elevate the Impact Eighty-Eight brand and amplify the message of this book.

To Arianna Leslie, the talented eye behind the look and feel of everything we create, your design work is more than aesthetics—it's an extension of our mission. Thank you for giving shape and color to our vision.

To Cassy Williamson, you have been a constant source of encouragement and inspiration. Your courage to write your book, *Unapologetic*, set the bar for me to follow. Watching you model vulnerability and leadership reminded me that every coach must also be a practitioner of growth.

To Lindsey Ayala, our chief growth officer—you are truly one of a kind. You took a chance on me, even when there wasn't a paycheck to go with it. You are the engine behind everything we do at Impact Eighty-Eight. I could not do this without your belief, your drive, and your brilliance.

To my family: Ashlee Nelson, not only are you the most amazing bonus daughter I could wish for, but you also happen to handle all the event planning for Impact Eighty-Eight. Every time we step on a stage or host a program, your touch ensures we look polished, professional, and unforgettable. Your company, Ashlee Nelson Curated Events (CuratedByAshlee.com) brings excellence to everything it touches. To my son-in-law, Zach Nelson, thank you for your encouragement and belief. It has meant more than you know.

And to my wife, Melissa—this book, and everything that has come before it, would not exist without you. Your love, your encouragement, and your unwavering belief are the fuel that keeps me going.

You are my partner in every sense, and I thank God every day for the gift of you.

Finally, I give thanks to God, who has blessed me with the gifts, guidance, and opportunities to do this work. May this book honor Him by equipping leaders to serve others well.

ABOUT THE AUTHOR

Ryan Taft is a speaker, author, and performance coach who helps leaders build sales teams that win. With more than twenty-five years of experience in sales, leadership, and coaching, Ryan has trained and coached thousands of professionals. His work focuses on real-world strategies that drive performance—not just in sales results, but in leadership, coaching, and team development.

Ryan's career path includes success as a top-producing salesperson, national sales trainer, and senior consultant. In 2024, he founded Impact Eighty-Eight, a performance improvement company that partners with organizations to elevate sales, coaching, leadership, and execution.

Ryan is also a Certified Speaking Professional (CSP) through the National Speakers Association (NSA), a designation held by fewer than eight hundred speakers worldwide, and a frequent contributor to podcasts, articles, and industry publications on the topics of sales, leadership, and performance improvement.

He is also the author of *The Sales Cure* and *StoryGetter* and coauthor of *Buying the Experience* and *Tougher Market New Home Sales*.

When he's not speaking or coaching, Ryan lives in Gilbert, Arizona, with his wife, Melissa, and their three dogs—Odie, Ava, and Chadwick.

READER'S NOTES

Growth happens when you translate learning into action, and the best way to do that is by writing it down.

These pages are here for you to use to capture the ideas, questions, and insights that hit you as you read or put the concepts of *RevenueGetter* into practice.

Use this space to record coaching breakthroughs, leadership reflections, quotes that resonate, or next steps you want to take.

Let these pages become a living record of your journey to becoming a true *RevenueGetter.*